THE MIRACLE OF AMERICAN INDEPENDENCE

THE MIRACLE OF AMERICAN INDEPENDENCE

TWENTY WAYS THINGS COULD HAVE TURNED OUT DIFFERENTLY

JONATHAN R. DULL

POTOMAC BOOKS
An imprint of the University of Nebraska Press

© 2015 by the Board of Regents of the University of Nebraska
All rights reserved. Potomac Books is an imprint of the
University of Nebraska Press.
Manufactured in the United States of America.

Library of Congress Cataloging-in-Publication Data
Dull, Jonathan R., 1942– author.
The miracle of American independence:
twenty ways things could have turned
out differently / Jonathan R. Dull.
pages   cm
Includes bibliographical references and index.
ISBN 978-1-61234-767-7 (pbk.: alk. paper)
ISBN 978-1-61234-780-6 (epub)
ISBN 978-1-61234-781-3 (mobi)
ISBN 978-1-61234-782-0 (pdf)
1. United States—History—
Revolution, 1775–1783. I. Title.
E208.D85 2015
973.3—dc23
2015024062

Set in Lyon Text by L. Auten.

CONTENTS

PREFACE

In the long run, American independence was not a miracle. The inhabitants of what is now the eastern half of the United States were so rapidly multiplying and the land they inhabited was so distant from Great Britain that eventually they would have become independent. The early timing of that independence and its huge extent, both political and territorial, however, do seem miraculous or close to it. The American Revolution might have been indefinitely postponed had British leaders been wiser or Americans less suspicious of them; I will discuss seven ways the revolution might have been averted. Once hostilities began, the British might have forced Americans back into obedience or at least forced them to accept less independence or less territory; I will examine a dozen turning points. These two sections are closely linked by a common theme: the disastrous results of British ignorance and arrogance. Finally I will look at the postwar fate of American independence.

There, of course, could be far more than twenty chapters in this book, because there are many things that could have happened differently. For example, the warship *Reprisal* sank during a storm on its return voyage from taking Benjamin Franklin to France in 1776; it could easily have happened during its voyage *to* France. How then did I make my selection? Partly it was on the basis on how possible it was that things could have happened other than they did, although in some cases (for example, chapter 7), the likelihood of a different outcome was small. Partly it was on the basis of the significance of a different outcome, although the stakes involved were not equally crucial; American independence might have survived a different outcome to the events in chapter 16, for example. As I wish to reach nonspecialists in the field, I also have selected topics that are not only important but also interesting for general readers (and in some cases relatively unfamiliar). I have paid particular attention to having the chapters flow into each other so as to form a unified narrative. I hope it will be a stimulating introduction or reintroduction to one of the most exciting periods in American and European history

I have drawn on my nearly fifty years of research and writing on the American Revolution and its "parent," the Seven Years' War (or, as it is frequently called in the United States, the French and Indian War). I have written seven previous books on French, British, and American history. The present book is a mixture of these national histories, the only way to do full justice to such a complex and interesting subject. I could not have written it without the support of my wonderful wife, Susan, and children, Max, Anna, Rob, and Veronica. I dedicate it to the memory of a wonderful man, my late father-in-law, Dr. Stanley Kruger.

Preface

THE MIRACLE OF AMERICAN INDEPENDENCE

1

Seven Ways the British Might Have Averted American Independence

ONE

Britain Could Have Continued to Accept America's Partial Autonomy

Most Americans who lived through the violence, misery, and terror of the American Revolution probably would have been happy if the peaceful and prosperous conditions of the 1720s and 1730s had never ended. This was a golden age in which the terrible wars between whites and Native Americans gradually ceased, at least for the moment, and the standard of living for both sets of people improved.[1] Europe, too, enjoyed a respite from the terrible wars that had plagued it during the previous decades. For the dozen years between 1721 and 1733, war virtually disappeared from the entire continent, the longest period of complete peace it had ever had. Even the climate improved. In the 1720s long-absent sunspots resumed, and the miserable cold years that marked the unhappy seventeenth century lost their hold over the Northern Hemisphere (and much of the rest of the world).[2] Famines and revolutions ceased to be common events, and the population of Europe increased, aided not only by the better climate but also by improved roads and canals by which food could be moved.[3] Plague became less of a threat as European states imposed widespread quarantines to prevent its spread; France saw its last major plague epidemic contained in 1720.

Meanwhile, many Americans and some Britons enjoyed not only peace and prosperity but also a large measure of self-government. The long struggle of political parties in Great Britain ended with the victory of the Whigs over the Tories. Between 1721 and 1743 First Lord of the Treasury (and unofficial prime minister) Robert Walpole commanded a solid majority in the House of Commons. Walpole loved peace, both domestic and foreign, and America benefited from the British government's benign indifference or, as Edmund Burke later called it, "salutary neglect."[4] In eight of the thirteen American colonies, Britain exerted its power through the governors appointed by the king upon the recommendation of Walpole's close ally Thomas Pelham-Hobbes, Duke of Newcastle, the secretary of state responsible for America. Governors generally were selected to reward Walpole's followers in the House of Commons and tended to share his desire not to rock the boat. In Pennsylvania, Maryland, and Delaware, the governor was appointed by a proprietor, a nobleman whose chief concern was enriching himself. Massachusetts and Connecticut selected their own governors. In spite of their differences, the colonies had in common a political life largely centered around an elected assembly, a lower house of the legislature that dominated the passage of legislation and levying of taxes.[5] The governor could veto legislation or the king's advisory Privy Council could disallow it, but for the most part these powers were exercised with a light hand. Britain, however, wielded considerable economic control over the colonies by regulating American industrial development, trade, and currency. Not all Americans were happy with being an economic satellite of Great Britain, but the mother country did provide markets for their exports (generally agricultural), credit for the functioning of their businesses and plantations, and the British-made consumer goods that they loved.

The colonists saw no contradiction in being simultaneously loyal to their local communities, their individual colonies, and their king. Gradually some came to think of themselves

America's Partial Autonomy

as Americans, although the definition was vague enough to sometimes include the colonists of the British West Indies. Americans had closer ties with Great Britain than with each other; America was large, communications were slow, and there were major religious, economic, and social differences among the colonies. The main connection among Americans was a rather good joint postal system and a network of newspapers. Each colony had its own militia, sometimes with a small British warship or two for protection from pirates. Each also generally maintained a lobbyist, called a colonial agent, in London. These tried to influence the Privy Council and its advisory committee, the Board of Trade, which approved their legislation, Parliament, which regulated their trade, and, in some cases, the secretary of state (a cabinet position), who appointed their governors.[6] What the colonies shared was loyalty to the crown, faith in the unwritten British constitution that apportioned power among the king, the House of Commons, and House of Lords, pride in being British, a dedication to self-government, and a mistrust of British politicians, government officials, and soldiers. Most American white men owned enough property to have the chance to vote, a privilege exercised by few Britons. Americans considered Parliament corrupt and government officials power-hungry and dangerous, whereas they were freer and hence more British than Britons themselves. As long as the British government left them alone, they could look down on Britain for its vices, while they traded with it, borrowed money from it, and tolerated its occasional intrusions into their lives. The British government in turn was willing to ignore the colonists' oddities, such as their lack of a landed nobility, as long as American trade contributed to Britain's prosperity and power.[7] Some Britons were concerned by the implications of America's amazing population growth, but as long as the British public and government paid little attention to America, "salutary neglect" worked well.

What brought an end to peaceful relations between Britain and America was the end of Britain's peaceful relations with Europe. The unprecedented European peace of 1721 to 1733 (which spread to the American frontier by the late 1720s) was based on an unusual combination of circumstances. After a long period of war such as that between 1688 and 1720, there generally was a short respite while the various former warring states rebuilt their finances. What enabled the present respite to last a dozen years was the unusual alliance of the three richest states in Europe: Great Britain, France, and the Netherlands (which then was called the United Provinces of the Netherlands to distinguish it from its southern neighbor, the Austrian Netherlands, now called Belgium). Not only were these three countries uninterested in fighting each other; they also were uninterested in financing wars in the rest of Europe. Moreover the wars of the previous quarter century had resolved a number of pressing issues such as whether Russia or Sweden would dominate eastern Europe. Russia won, but it was not yet on the same level as the three great powers of Europe: Britain, France, and Austria. These wars greatly diminished the relative standing of other countries like Spain, Sweden, and the rich but militarily weak Netherlands. Most international issues could now be resolved by intimidation or negotiation, and a series of diplomatic conferences (called "congresses," a distant forerunner of the United Nations) was set up to resolve them.[8]

Unfortunately, this peaceful system was unstable. The English public generally disliked and mistrusted France, which was Catholic and had fought England for more than twenty years after the "Glorious Revolution" of 1688 deposed King James II of England, a Catholic and a cousin of the king of France.[9] The British government still feared a French invasion even though the French navy was only a fraction of the size of the British and virtually stopped building new ships in the late 1720s.[10] Perhaps most important, the leaders who had negotiated the Franco-British alliance died during the 1720s. The new French leader, young King Louis XV's tutor, Cardinal André-Hercule de Fleury, was as prudent as were Walpole and Newcastle, but King George II, who assumed the English throne in 1727, saw little value in the French alliance. In 1731 he negotiated an alliance with France's longstanding rival, Austria. In response, France allied with Spain.[11]

In 1733 war returned to Europe as France and Russia backed rival claimants to the throne of Poland. Austria joined the war as an ally of Russia, while Spain joined it as an ally of France. Britain remained neutral, and France took care not to threaten British security. It refrained from invading the Austrian Netherlands (from which an invasion of England could be launched) and sent only a tiny squadron to fight the Russians in the Baltic Sea. Thus the war had no impact in America.[12]

In 1739, Britain declared war on its colonial rival, Spain, which did affect America. War broke out on the frontier between Georgia and Spanish Florida, while thousands of Americans volunteered for a British expedition in the Caribbean (which was defeated).[13] France remained neutral. The following year, the ruler of Austria died. He had been the Holy Roman emperor, a title that in theory made him the ruler of Germany (which in practical terms meant only where people spoke German) but in fact had little real power. His heir, his daughter Maria Theresa, was not eligible to be elected Holy Roman emperor. Her real inheritance was the lands directly ruled by her family, the Habsburgs: Austria, the Austrian Netherlands, Hungary, Bohemia, and significant other possessions in Italy, Germany, and eastern Europe. Various rulers of Europe, including Louis XV, had promised to respect her right to inherit them, but one greedy ruler, Frederick II of Prussia, a medium-sized state in northern Germany, invaded Silesia, an Austrian province that today is part of Poland. Louis XV was now thirty years old and chose not to listen to Cardinal Fleury's advice to disregard Prussia's offer of an alliance against Austria. Instead he decided to join in the plunder, hoping to so weaken Austria that it would never again pose a threat to France. Soon Britain came to the assistance of Maria Theresa and went to war against France.[14]

Louis's dishonorable decision would affect not only his reign but also that of his grandson and successor, Louis XVI. It undercut the security of promises and the rule of law in international relations. It helped make European diplomacy a jungle ruled by violence despite the eighteenth century's reputation as being a period of limited wars. The ensuing War of the Austrian Succession led to two more wars, the Seven Years' War and the War of American Independence, that bankrupted the French monarchy and led to the French Revolution. It also poisoned relations with Great Britain for the next seventy years; on several occasions during those years France tried to reestablish good relations, only for its offers to be rejected by British governments unwilling to brave the English public's hostility to France. The war also spilled over into North America with disastrous consequences.

The outbreak of fighting along the American frontier in 1745 ended a generation of uneasy peace between white British colonists and Native Americans. Moreover, the war, called in America "King George's War," led to a split among the Iroquois confederation of six Native American nations in northern and western New York. Hitherto the confederation had served as a buffer between French Canada and the upper British colonies. Now the Mohawks, the easternmost Iroquois nation, went to war on behalf of the British and attempted a raid on Montreal. Tension also increased because the British navy's blockade of shipping from France cut the French supply line to its native allies in the Great Lakes area, the Upper Country or *pays d'en haut*. As the traditional Native American alliances with the French weakened, a power vacuum was created in the western part of Pennsylvania. British American traders flooded the areas, whose borders were in dispute. The war fostered British Americans' fear of Native Americans and increased their desire for Native American land.[15]

The most important military action in North America was on Cape Breton Island, where the French had built Louisbourg, a fortified port city used to support the French fishing boats using the Newfoundland and St. Lawrence fisheries, regarded as vital for training sailors for the French navy. In 1745 a volunteer army from New England supported by units of the British navy captured Louisbourg. At the end of the War of the Austrian Succession in 1748, Louisbourg was returned to France. The French in turn evacuated the Austrian Netherlands, which their army had captured. American colonists were outraged at what they regarded as a betrayal by British negotiators at the peace conference (held in the German city of Aix-la-Chapelle). Thus the war created suspicion in America that the British neglect of them was not benign but rather reflected indifference toward their contributions.[16]

The war also made a difference in British attitudes. It had been expensive for Britain as well as for France. Within the British government there were now those who believed that the administration of the American colonies needed to be more efficient. Americans blackmailed royal governors by threatening to withhold their salaries, they evaded British trade regulations by smuggling with the French West Indies, and they contributed almost nothing to the royal treasury. Resentment of the Americans' semi-independence was particularly strong among the members of the Board of Trade (which issued the instructions to royal governors), especially its chairman, George Montagu Dunk, Earl of Halifax. For the moment they could not overcome the weight of government inertia, but their desire to change the system of salutary neglect was ominous.[17] So too was the departure of Walpole, a victim of the public's aggressiveness born of the war. Although Walpole was despised in America for his supposed corruption and pursuit of power, he had been the main support for the loose system of administering America. Ominous, too, was the huge rise of the British national debt,[18] which weakened British tolerance for America's not paying a share of Britain's heavy taxes. The war also had weakened the Iroquois confederation as a force for peace, undermined the uneasy tolerance between whites and Native Americans, and threatened Native American hunting grounds, which never had been completely safe from the colonists' land hunger. Perhaps most dangerous of all, it had poisoned British relations with France and made more contentious their conflicting claims along the never defined border of French-speaking Acadia (now New Brunswick and Nova Scotia) and the border between the British colonies and Canada, particularly the area around the headwaters of the Ohio River. The Treaty of Aix-la-Chapelle, like the Treaty of Utrecht of 1713, left border issues to be resolved by a joint British-French border commission, but its success would depend on the willingness of Louis XV, George II, and their governments to compromise.

Thus the Franco-British war of 1744–48 inflicted a dangerous wound on the system of salutary neglect, the British policy of looking the other way and accommodating the actions, aspirations, and fears of their American colonists. Its survival would require turning the clock back to the 1720s and 1730s. Had the British been able to do so, there would have been little reason for Americans to consider changing a relationship that was less one of dependence and subordination than one of a mutually beneficial partnership. Unfortunately the survival of that partnership was less a question of British-American relations than it was of Britain's relations with France. On those relations hinged the survival of Britain's policy of salutary neglect of its colonies.

TWO

There Might Have Been a Peaceful Resolution of the Colonial Rivalry of 1748-1755

Under the odd division of responsibility in place until 1782, British foreign and colonial policy was split between a secretary of state for the north, responsible for implementing British policy toward the great powers of eastern Europe (now including Prussia), and a secretary of state for the south, responsible for relations with France, Spain, and the American colonies (among other places). Thus the most important person in dealing with both France and the American colonies was the southern secretary, the Duke of Newcastle. It is hard to imagine a less menacing or tyrannical figure than the dithering and kindly (although jealous of potential rivals) Newcastle, whose genius was in the subtle arts of patronage and political management.[1] Newcastle's failings as a statesman were not extremism or aggression but his insularity, his inability to see things from, for example, a French perspective. It would be an exaggeration to say that the war that began in 1754-55 was a simple misunderstanding, as there were genuine conflicts involved, particularly concerning America's borders. Newcastle, however, misjudged France's foreign policy goals, exaggerated the French threat, and missed a chance to reduce the tensions that led to war. Some Frenchmen, particularly in the foreign ministry, were open to accommodation with Britain, but they had little chance of overcoming the obstacles to the one way that

Britain and France could have been spared from an even more disastrous war than the previous one—a return to the Franco-British cooperation of the 1720s and early 1730s. In the process the British policy of salutary neglect of its colonies might also have been saved.

Newcastle did have reason to be suspicious of King Louis XV and his government. During the last war France had broken its promise to recognize Maria Theresa's right of inheritance, had attacked Britain in 1744 before declaring war, had tried to invade England, had threatened Britain by capturing the Austrian Netherlands, and had supported the Scottish uprising of 1745 on behalf of James II's descendants. France, however, now had achieved its basic goal. It had indirectly weakened Austria by raising Prussia as a counterweight in the Holy Roman Empire because of its conquest of Silesia, the one conquest of any power not restored at the Treaty of Aix-la-Chapelle. France thus became, like Britain, a satisfied power that wanted no further changes to the map of Europe. Although still rivals in America, Britain and France became natural allies in Europe; to a continental power like France, this was far more important than possessing colonies. Some French diplomats also realized that the best peace treaty is one that enables you to reconcile with your former enemies (as the United States did with Germany, Italy, and Japan after 1945). Furthermore, France had a very good reason for better relations with Britain. The war had created a new enemy on the European continent for France in place of Austria. In 1748 France had been quick to sign a moderate peace partly because a Russian army hired by the British was marching across central Europe to the rescue of the Netherlands. Louis-Philogène Brûlart, marquis de Puyzieulx, the wise French foreign minister in 1748, realized the ongoing Russian threat. The Russians menaced the outer ring of France's defenses, the large but weak states of Sweden, Poland, and the Ottoman Empire (which included Turkey and the Balkans). (The inner ring was Spain plus small states in Germany, Italy, and Switzerland, many of whom were subsidized by France.) After the war was over, he began constructing a series of anti-Russian defensive alliances.[2] There was no way Newcastle could have joined in, even had he trusted France; English public opinion was so embittered that cooperation was impossible.

Another difficulty was that neither Newcastle nor Puyzieulx and his successors at the French foreign ministry had a free hand. Newcastle had opponents such as Halifax in high places, while the French foreign ministers had rivals in Louis XV's council of state, particularly the secretary of state for naval and colonial affairs, Antoine-Louis Rouillé. Halifax and his friends, as well as Rouillé and his subordinates, were obsessed with the disputes in North America and regarded each other's nation as a major threat. Indeed fear was the common denominator in North America: Native American fears of white encroachment, French fears of losing their native alliances in the Upper Country, British and American fears that the French would permanently pin the British colonies east of the Appalachian Mountains, fears of the British authorities who had governed Acadia for the last forty years that its French-speaking population would try to return it to French control, and Acadian fears that the British would no longer permit them to remain neutral in case of another French-British conflict.

A series of events after 1748 added to these fears. The British established a new settlement and naval base named Halifax in Acadia, to which they brought colonists. This invasion of their hunting grounds outraged the Mi'kmaq nation, who had long enjoyed good relations, including intermarriage, with their French-speaking neighbors. They responded by attacking colonists, thereby increasing British suspicion of the Acadians. Meanwhile, the Acadians came under French pressure to move to the part of Acadia west of the Missaguash River, where there were no British. (This river today forms the border between New Brunswick and Nova Scotia, the British name for eastern Acadia.) The British built Fort Lawrence on the east bank of the river, while the French built Fort Beauséjour on the west bank. This temporarily stabilized the situation, but tensions remained high.[3]

The situation was also dangerous in the area where the Allegheny and Monongahela Rivers join to form the Ohio River (at the site of today's Pittsburgh). A series of inexperienced governors general at Quebec chose to use force against the British American traders in the area rather than competing with them economically by generously subsidizing their own trade goods. In 1752 a French and Native American war party burned Pickawillany, a Native American village near today's Piqua, Ohio, used by British traders, and killed its headman. Meanwhile a number of competing British and American land speculators made plans to form settlements in the area. One group of Virginia speculators called the Ohio Company built a fortified trading post on the upper Potomac River and began planning to build another at the forks of the Ohio. The successive governors general, although not fully aware of the Ohio Company's intentions, became convinced that the British wished to cut the lake and river connection between French Canada and French Louisiana. One of them, Ange Duquesne de Menneville, marquis Duquesne, acted on instructions from Rouillé to drive the British from the area. He drafted Canadian militiamen and began constructing a string of forts from Lake Erie to the very spot where the Ohio Company planned to build its new fortified trading post and settlement. In late 1753 the Ohio Company sent a young surveyor named George Washington to one of the French forts to warn the French to withdraw. A confrontation loomed even though this area produced few furs, the major export of a Canada that did not even pay the cost of administering it. The French fort building aroused the resentment of the reluctant Canadian militiamen as well as the Delaware and Shawnee, who had not given the French permission to invade their hunting grounds. The Ohio Company in turn pressed on in spite of its growing expenses to settle an area to which Pennsylvania had a stronger claim than did Virginia.

Both sides were responsible for the growing danger. Rouillé was a narrow-minded bureaucrat who knew little about Canada and hence was easily won over by the exaggerated fears communicated by the governors general. (The main route between the St. Lawrence and Mississippi Rivers was in fact well to the west along the Maumee, Wabash, and Ohio Rivers.) The Ohio Company's investors were motivated only by greed. Their grandiose plans would have collapsed on their own or would have met with strong Native American resistance had they not led to a confrontation with the French.[4] Could nothing have been done to stop the rush to disaster?

The only hope was a peaceful settlement between Louis XV and George II, possibly including the disputed Caribbean islands of Dominica, St. Vincent, St. Lucia, Tobago, and Grenada. The chances of such a settlement were not helped by the bilateral border commission reestablished by the Treaty of Aix-la-Chapelle to peacefully settle disputes.[5] Unfortunately the British and French governments appointed the worst possible commissioners. The British appointments included Massachusetts governor William Shirley, a rabid expansionist who wanted to drive the Acadians from their homes and replace them with New Englanders. The French appointments included former acting governor general Roland-Michel Barrin, marquis de La Galissonière, the principal purveyor of the supposed British threat to the Canada-Louisiana link. The bilateral commission became a debating society that merely inflamed the controversy. The French claimed all the land west of the Allegheny Mountains, while the British claimed all the lands that ever belonged to the Iroquois who, according to the 1713 Treaty of Utrecht, were British dependents.

Little hope could be placed in Louis XV, even though the last war had been a disillusioning experience for this basically kindhearted and sentimental man, who did not want another war. He was still too immature and lacking in self-confidence to exercise control over his own government, but he was unwilling to subject himself to another chief minister like Fleury. Thus he let the foreign and naval ministries pursue contradictory policies. Compounding the problem, the foreign minister died in July 1754 and was replaced by the ineffectual Rouillé. The new naval and colonial minister was the French finance minister, Jean-Baptiste de Machault d' Arnouville. Machault soon proved a brilliant naval minister, but he knew nothing about the French colonies and played little part in the attempt to prevent war.[6]

George II was no more helpful.[7] He was not only king of England and ruler of Scotland and Ireland but also ruler of a medium-sized principality in northern Germany, the electorate of Hanover. (It was called an electorate because its ruler was an elector, one of the nine rulers who elected each Holy Roman emperor, whose tenure was for life.) George was well versed in diplomacy, but, born in Germany, he was not an expert in trade and colonial issues in general and America in particular. Unfortunately he turned for advice to his favorite son, William Augustus, Duke of Cumberland, the head of the British army. Cumberland was an aggressive man who had won his reputation by his brutal repression of the Scottish rebellion of 1745. He was as eager for a new war (so as to increase his glory) as was the Earl of Halifax, head of the Board of Trade, who wished to increase his leverage over the American colonists. They worked together to undercut the new British prime minister, the Duke of Newcastle, who did not want war.

The crisis finally came in 1754. It happened not because of malevolence but because of incompetence. In 1754 the French fort builders and the Ohio Company raced to be first to the

Colonial Rivalry of 1748–1755

forks of the Ohio. The Virginians won, but they had only forty men. When 600 Canadians arrived, they peacefully abandoned their partially built fort and even sold the Canadians their tools. This takeover outraged the acting governor of Virginia, Robert Dinwiddie, who was a major investor in the Ohio Company. He persuaded the Virginia House of Burgesses to finance an expedition to take back the site. Once again the Virginians' action was both provocative and ineffectual. They sent 200 untried soldiers led by the immature and inexperienced George Washington. As they approached the French camp, Washington, fearing an ambush, led a patrol of 50 soldiers and Native Americans, including Tanaghrisson, an Iroquois who wished to start hostilities for his own self-interest. On May 28 Washington's party encountered a 35-man Canadian patrol that been sent to warn the Virginians to leave. It was the Canadians who were taken by surprise. In a brief skirmish a dozen of them were killed, including their commander, young Ensign Joseph Coulon de Villiers de Jumonville. Tanaghrisson murdered him after he surrendered (for which the French government would blame Washington). The Virginians fled and built a stockade nearby that they called Fort Necessity, while they awaited reinforcements. Not enough came before a detachment of 700 Canadians and Native Americans arrived, commanded by Jumonville's brother. After a one-sided battle, the Virginians surrendered and were allowed to return home. Washington did not read the surrender terms closely enough and inadvertently admitted to assassinating Jumonville.[8]

This sordid affair inflamed public opinion in both Britain and France.[9] To mollify British public opinion, Newcastle tried to negotiate a border settlement with France, while also sending troops from the British army to seize the forks of the Ohio. Unwisely he used the Duke of Cumberland to win his father's consent to send the troops.[10] Newcastle hoped to force the French into a satisfactory border agreement by gradually applying pressure. Instead Cumberland and Halifax ruined Newcastle's cautious plan. They speeded up the process, expanded the size of the force and its objectives, and publicized the troops' departure in order to make a compromise difficult. As the two sides prepared to negotiate, there was a stroke of bad fortune. William Keppel, Earl of Albemarle, the veteran British ambassador at the French court who earlier had praised Puyzieulx, died unexpectedly.[11] Negotiations were then conducted by the French ambassador at the British court and Newcastle's secretary of state for the southern department. The main parties to the negotiations actually were Newcastle himself and Rouillé, the pedantic and self-righteous French foreign minister back at the French court. Any hope of their success was sabotaged by the war party at the British court. After Newcastle submitted his proposal for the border of the Ohio country, he was forced to withdraw it and submit less generous terms. Louis XV was outraged at what he saw as trickery. Under the circumstances France could have broken off negotiations, but Rouillé continued the discussions, which became an exercise in self-justification like the exchange of memoranda during the sterile border commission discussions. Meanwhile both sides prepared military and naval forces for North America.

In retrospect France's only hope was accepting whatever conditions Newcastle offered. Canada, which barely grew enough food to feed itself, could not support enough troops for its own defense. The French navy was completely unprepared for war.[12] Its only allies were Spain, ruled by an ineffectual king who was unwilling to fight, and Prussia, which during the last war had twice betrayed France to make separate peace agreements with Austria. Moreover the fifteen-year alliance signed with Prussia at the beginning of the last war was due to expire in July 1756. Louis nevertheless was unable to avoid war once negotiations failed because of his sense of honor and his fear of losing face and thereby weakening the alliances on which French security depended. Britain in contrast was ready for a war in which *all* the North American border issues could be settled before France could fight back. This was ominously like the British plan to despoil Spain in 1739 or the French plan of 1741 to permanently solve the Austrian problem. Wars are seldom as easy as they appear. This war, too, would be long, bloody, and ruinously expensive. In the process it would make impossible not only the return of good relations with France but also the resumption of the policy of salutary neglect that had so well served both America and Britain. During the war Britain and America cooperated successfully, and at war's end British-American relations seemed to be on a good footing, but in the long run, the war poisoned their relationship. The best hope for returning to the stable relations of the 1720s and 1730s had been to avoid a new war after 1748 so that gradually things could return to normal. The fears and suspicions born of the war of 1744–48 proved too strong to overcome, though, in spite of the goodwill of statesmen like Puyzieulx. All that could be hoped now was that the new war would be quick and decisive so as not to further disrupt Britain's relationship with its North American colonies.

THREE

The War of 1755 Could Have Ended
in a Quick British Victory

The coming war would end after eight years in a seemingly total British victory. The British and their colonial subjects not only conquered Canada but even drove the French almost completely from North America. This result was not inevitable. British objectives shifted over the course of the war, and only after Canada was captured did the British decide to keep it. Even before the war started, British war objectives began expanding. Newcastle simply wanted to resolve the dispute over the headwaters of the Ohio River, although he was ready to expand progressively the military means to attain it.[1] Cumberland and Halifax had a much wider agenda that they convinced George II to accept. They aimed at eliminating France's presence from south of the St. Lawrence River and Lakes Ontario and Erie. This included Acadia, the area around the Bay of Fundy, but left open the question of the Upper Country, particularly French Detroit and the Illinois country. Had the British quickly achieved a peace giving them their wishes, many of the war's consequences could have been avoided: the spread of the war to Europe, the huge rise in the British national debt, the tensions with the colonies caused by the eventual sending of tens of thousands of British troops to America, and the war's most dangerous legacy, the retention of 10,000 troops in America at the end of the conflict.

The change in war objectives dictated an increase in the resources devoted to achieving them. Newcastle's plan was to send to the forks of the Ohio two regiments currently stationed in Ireland. After being brought to full strength by recruiting in America, they would total more than 1,500 men. Should France not immediately give in, Newcastle believed it would be sufficient to capture progressively the main French posts in areas claimed by Britain and its colonies: Fort Niagara on the Niagara River where it entered Lake Ontario, Fort St. Frédéric on Lake Champlain, and Fort Beauséjour plus a smaller nearby fort in Acadia. Excluding the 1,200 troops at Louisbourg, which was not targeted, the French had only 1,500 marines (sometimes called colonial regulars) in Canada; these were furnished by the naval and colonial ministry and consisted of French troops and Canadian officers who were accustomed to fighting alongside Native American allies. The new British plans called for recruiting two more regiments in the colonies and for using troops already in Acadia plus 2,000 volunteers from New England to capture Fort Beauséjour and the other nearby fort. The British government was so confident of success that it rejected a plan proposed by Benjamin Franklin for a military union of the American colonies; this plan was adopted at a conference in Albany dealing with Iroquois grievances, but received no support from colonial legislatures.[2]

Louis XV responded to the British preparations by taking countermeasures to protect Canada, but in moderation so as not to be provocative. The French army provided 2,400 troops for Quebec and 1,200 for Louisbourg. To save time, the navy elected not to hire transports. Instead, most of the cannon were removed from nine elderly ships of the line so they could be used to carry the troops. (Normally a ship of the line carried 60 to 100 cannon.) Four ships of the line would accompany them across the Atlantic while a larger body of ships would escort them clear of the French coast and then return to the departure point, the great naval base of Brest at the tip of Brittany. All these ships sailed from Brest on May 3, 1755. Such a tiny military and naval force was not a threat to the American colonies, whose population outnumbered Canada's 60,000 or 70,000 inhabitants by twenty to one.[3]

The British were unwilling to allow the French reinforcements to disrupt their various offensives. On April 27, 1755, a squadron of eleven fully armed ships of the line commanded by Admiral Edward Boscawen sailed from England for the waters off the entrance of the St. Lawrence River. His orders were to intercept French warships and transports and to capture or destroy them if they resisted. This attack without a declaration of war was a mirror image of the French attack on Britain in 1744 and, like it, was perceived as treacherous and left a long-standing residue of bitterness. On June 10 Boscawen's squadron intercepted the French, but most of their ships were shielded by fog and escaped detection. The British found only two of the converted transports and one of the escorts. They captured the transport *Lys* and the escort *Alcide* after telling them that Britain and France were still at peace. The other transport escaped, and virtually all the troops reached Louisbourg and Quebec City safely. Aboard the ships arriving at Quebec on June 23 were the veteran commander of the detachment of army troops, Jean Erdmann, baron de Dieskau, and a new governor general, Pierre de Rigaud de Vaudreuil de Cavagnial, marquis de Vaudreuil.[4]

As Boscawen was beginning hostilities at sea, troops were already marching to attack Fort Beauséjour and Fort Duquesne, the new French fort at the forks of the Ohio. It took only a few days to capture Fort Beauséjour and the smaller nearby fort. The nearly bloodless offensive was followed by an atrocity that embittered Frenchmen and Canadians even more than had the killing of Jumonville or Boscawen's unprovoked attack. After waiting for the French-speaking Acadians to complete their harvest, the British seized their crops and homes and put all of the Acadian men, women, and children that they could find aboard ships. Many Acadians were separated from their neighbors and sometimes from family members and then were scattered among the various American colonies, where they were unwelcome. Some 6,000 or 7,000 were rounded up and shipped away, almost half the population of Acadia; the remainder were already west of Fort Beauséjour or escaped. Some of the exiles died, but many (called "Cajuns," a corruption of "Acadians") eventually found their way to Louisiana. Such brutal treatment was customary toward Native Americans but considered shameful when dealing with fellow Europeans. Britons defended it as self-protection, even though the tolerant and peace-loving Acadians posed no military threat and their Mi'kmaq friends only a minor one.[5]

Fort Duquesne met a different fate. The troops from Ireland arrived in Virginia in March under the escort of two 50-gun ships (intermediate in size between a ship of the line and a frigate of 20 to 44 cannon). The following month their commander, General Edward Braddock, met at Alexandria with the governors or acting governors of Virginia, Maryland, New York, Massachusetts, and Pennsylvania. The meeting went poorly. Braddock had little combat experience, but Cumberland seems to have chosen him because he was a kindred spirit, an arrogant, aggressive, and peremptory bully. Rather than seek the governors' cooperation, he ordered them to provide him with money and whatever other support he needed. Not surprisingly, they were not very helpful. It took the intervention of Pennsylvania assemblyman Benjamin Franklin to procure for Braddock the draft animals, wagons, and teamsters he needed to support his army's 100-mile march to Fort Duquesne from his base camp at Fort Cumberland, Maryland. By the time they reached his camp, Braddock had recruited enough soldiers to complete his regiments.

The army that left camp on May 29 was very unwieldy. It

had 2,200 soldiers, including 400 Virginia, Maryland, and North Carolina provincial troops (troops recruited annually by colonial governments), 29 artillery pieces to besiege Fort Duquesne if it proved necessary, and a huge baggage train. It had only a handful of Native Americans for scouting, though, as Braddock's contempt had driven most of them away. His progress north across the mountains was barely two miles a day, as he had to construct a road for cannon and baggage. To speed his march he split his force, taking 1,500 picked troops ahead and leaving the rest to follow.

On July 9 his advance force forded without opposition the Monongahela River a few miles south of Fort Duquesne. As the forest thinned, Braddock grew overconfident. He had done no scouting and failed to make sure that his subordinate, Lieutenant Colonel Thomas Gage, occupied a hill along his march route. As he approached the fort, the defenders attacked him. When Braddock's march began, there had been only 600 marines and Canadian militia at the flimsy fort, but his slow progress had given 600 allied Native Americans time to arrive. Realizing that the fort could not withstand a siege, the Canadian commander sent half of his militia and marines to attack the approaching British column. Their headlong assault was repulsed and the commander of the detachment killed. They were accompanied, however, by virtually all of their Native American allies, who fired from cover on the British. The British advance guard fell back 100 yards where it collided with the main body of the oncoming British troops. Jammed together and confused by the unfamiliar Native American tactics, almost two-thirds of the soldiers and virtually all of their officers were killed or wounded, many by friendly fire. (Washington, a volunteer on Braddock's staff, miraculously escaped injury.) With Braddock mortally wounded, they finally retreated. When they reached their slower colleagues two days later, they transmitted their panic. Some 1,300 men reassembled at Fort Cumberland, but then continued to Philadelphia, where their temporary commander requested winter quarters.[6] Meanwhile Shawnee and Delaware raiding parties began attacking settlements on the now undefended frontier.[7]

Braddock's defeat had an impact on the other British offensives. His written plans for the other campaigns were captured and sent to Governor General Vaudreuil. The British could not have encountered a more dangerous opponent. Although an admiral in the French navy (like previous governors general), Vaudreuil, himself the son of a former governor general, was Canadian by birth, experience, and sympathy. As a young man he had fought in the Upper Country against an unfriendly nation, the Fox. He later served as governor of Louisiana. He viewed Native Americans not as savages but as useful allies. Although his private life was blameless, he was a ruthless warrior with an unparalleled knowledge of American and Canadian geography and a grudge against the British for their actions in Acadia.[8]

Vaudreuil's first thought was to protect Fort Niagara lest the supply route to the Upper Country be cut. He received intelligence, though, that the greatest threat was to Fort St. Frédéric on Lake Champlain. This was confirmed by the campaign plans captured from Braddock. Therefore he sent a large detachment under Dieskau to Lake Champlain.

The British, meanwhile, made another blunder. Governor Shirley, who succeeded Braddock as the acting army commander in America, logically should have commanded the army of mostly New England provincial troops assembling at Albany to attack Fort St. Frédéric. Anxious for the glory of capturing Fort Niagara, he instead assumed command of the two new army regiments ordered to march from Albany through Iroquois territory to the New York colony fortified trading post of Oswego on Lake Ontario, where they would build boats to take them to Fort Niagara. As a consolation prize, he gave command of the Lake Champlain expedition to William Johnson, an Irishman who spoke Mohawk and had a Mohawk common-law wife. Johnson was trusted by the Mohawks, but at heart he was a Briton and a selfish and unscrupulous one at that. Johnson and his Iroquois friends gave no help to Shirley's troops, who arrived at Oswego too late to advance further before the onset of winter.[9]

Meanwhile Johnson's 3,500 provincial troops and 300 Mohawks arrived at the south shore of Lake George at about the same time as Dieskau reached Lake Champlain, into which Lake George flows at its northern end via a short connecting stream. With Dieskau were 1,500 marines and militia, 800 army troops, and 700 Native Americans. He split his forces just as Braddock had done, taking ahead 1,500 picked men, half of them Native Americans, via a circuitous route to Lake George. As he approached the British camp on September 8, he encountered a large patrol sent out by Johnson. He was unable to surprise them because his Mohawks sounded a warning to the Mohawks serving with Johnson. Dieskau pursued the retreating Americans and pro-British Mohawks to the British camp where Johnson had erected a barricade. Doubtless to the astonishment of the Indians (who preferred inflicting casualties to taking them), Dieskau used his 200 army regulars in a frontal assault that was repulsed. Both Johnson and Dieskau were wounded, and Dieskau was captured; he and Johnson became friends during their recuperation. Both sides had suffered several hundred casualties, and the season was growing late. The French returned to Lake Champlain, where they built a new fort, Fort Carillon, south of Fort St. Frédéric. The British in turn began a fort, Fort William Henry, at the site of the battle.[10]

The botched opening campaign was humiliating for the British army. Before his defeat Braddock had insulted not only his Indian allies but also the American colonists. Then his defeated army abandoned the frontier to hide in Philadelphia. In contrast, Johnson's Americans had beaten back an enemy attack, and New England volunteers had provided most of the troops used to capture the forts on the border of eastern Acadia. New Englanders now rushed to take over the farms seized from the Acadians.[11]

Although Americans viewed themselves, not without reason, as better at wilderness fighting than were the British, they would need British troops against Vaudreuil's regulars, marines, and Native American allies. They did not receive many in time for the 1756 campaign. The British army was small by European standards and needed time to expand. The British did send two more regiments from Ireland and began raising a double-sized regiment of foreign immigrants in Pennsylvania and neighboring colonies. The French sent two more battalions (half regiments) safely to Canada in 1756, as well as a replacement for Dieskau. The new French army commander was an artillery specialist from southern France, Louis-Joseph, marquis de Montcalm-Gozon de St. Véran. Although a competent director of siege operations and a decent man appalled by the brutality of war in North America, Montcalm was a poor choice. He was rigid, conventional, and overly cautious, as well as being prejudiced against Canadians and Native Americans.[12]

His first campaign, however, was successful, largely because Vaudreuil overruled his objections and sent him on a daring attack that captured Oswego and its garrison.[13] The British planned a huge attack on Fort Carillon, but it was doomed by various delays including the wait for a new commander, John Campbell, Earl of Loudoun, another protégé of Cumberland. This futile second campaign ended what little hope remained for a quick victory in North America. Loudoun, although more intelligent than Braddock, was almost as tactless and soon became involved in disputes with the colonists about providing housing for his troops. This, too, did not bode well for a return to the relaxed relations of the period of salutary neglect.[14]

The British also missed an opportunity in the waters off the great French merchant ports of Le Havre, Rouen, Nantes, and Bordeaux. The French navy, like the British, could not afford to train its own sailors during peacetime. When war broke out, it made use of sailors trained aboard fishing boats and merchant ships. Although the British made greater use of sailors arriving from overseas aboard merchant ships, such sailors also were vital to the French. Had the British captured enough arriving merchant ships before war was declared, they could have crippled the French navy.

Naval Minister Machault devised a brilliant plan to foil the British. In June 1755 he sent a small squadron of his best ships of the line on a courtesy visit to Lisbon and then stationed them off the northwest coast of Spain. The British did not know whether the French planned to intercept Britain's own incoming shipping or whether they might even use the squadron to escort a French landing party to England. They also did not want to fire the first shot in European waters, giving the Dutch an excuse not to honor their defensive alliance with Britain. The French squadron did something unexpected. It did not attack. When it captured a British frigate, it promptly released it. The confused British waited until late summer to order the commander of its home fleet to take French prizes. The British finally captured hundreds of ships and 7,500 crewmen, but most of the incoming ships arrived safely. (Outgoing ships knew not to leave port.) All but one of the surviving ships that had taken the reinforcements to Louisbourg and Quebec returned safely. The astute French admiral took a seldom used route to evade the British at the mouth of the St. Lawrence and then took advantage of British confusion to reach port.[15] At the beginning of 1756, the naval momentum shifted in France's favor, dealing another terrible blow to British hopes for a quick victory.

The War of 1755

FOUR

The French Could Have Won the War

The stalemate in America gave France a good opportunity to win the war against Britain in Europe. Had it done so, the American Revolution would have been long delayed.

By the late summer of 1755, the French court realized that a war with Britain was almost inevitable.[1] Louis XV's council of state seems to have agreed that France must fight lest it suffer unacceptable damage to its reputation and thereby its own security and that of its allies. It also agreed that France would have to conquer something in Europe to counterbalance its losses in North America. Canada did not grow enough food or import enough from France to support more than a delaying action, whereas the British colonies to its south grew surpluses large enough to feed however large an army it took to defeat the French, Canadians, and Native Americans. The debate among Louis's advisors therefore was about how to force Britain to grant acceptable peace terms. There were two alternatives. First, France could again conquer the Austrian Netherlands, whose ports posed a danger to the defense of the English coast. This, however, would require an ally. Although King Frederick II of Prussia had fewer than 4 million subjects, his superb army made him an equal match for Maria Theresa and her 15 million subjects. (France had a population of 24 million, Russia about 20 million, Great Britain and Ireland about 11 million). Unfortunately he had proven an unreliable ally, twice abandoning France during the last war. What is more, the Franco-Prussian alliance was due to expire in July 1756. Maria Theresa in contrast signaled her willingness to befriend France by *reducing* her garrison in the Austrian Netherlands. Her chief advisor, Graf Wenzel Anton von Kautnitz-Rietberg, a former ambassador to the French court, was an advocate of using a French alliance to attack Prussia and regain Silesia.

The alternative to attacking the Austrian Netherlands was attacking George II's beloved electorate of Hanover. Although technically the British government was not obliged to defend it, there was no chance Parliament would neglect the king's wishes. Moreover, Hanover gave entrance to two of the major rivers of Germany, the Elbe and the Weser, facilitating British trade with numerous German principalities.

Attacking Hanover, though, presented its own problems. It would necessitate making an alliance with Austria. The Austrian Netherlands were dangerously near the route a French army must take to reach Hanover, whose southern border was 200 miles from anywhere in France. Even more important, Louis would need the help of Maria Theresa and her amiable mediocrity of a husband, Holy Roman Emperor Francis I, to obtain transit rights through the principalities along the way. Perhaps most important, he would need the consent of the Holy Roman Empire, which still had important judicial functions, to prevent Catholic France's invasion of Protestant Hanover from turning into a religious war convulsing Germany.[2] Maria Theresa had little sympathy for France's invading the territory of a fellow elector. In exchange she surely would demand that France help her regain Silesia. Not only would this mean a massive expansion of the war, but it was liable to undo the one accomplishment of the previous war, the creation of a balance of power in central Europe between Austria and Prussia. It also would mean reversing two cen-

France Could Have Won the War

turies of French opposition to the growth in power of Maria Theresa's family, the Habsburgs.

Louis wisely took his time making such a momentous decision, keeping his options open as long as possible. He informed Maria Theresa he would not invade the Austrian Netherlands, but he did send a prestigious envoy to Prussia to discuss renewing their alliance. He also sent peace feelers to George II, but without success.[3]

Britain had its own difficulties. The British navy could defend the British Isles from invasion, but could do little to protect Hanover. The Hanoverians, like the Acadians, wished only to live in peace, but they were victims of the historical accident that their ruler also was king of England. They had escaped the previous war, but unless Britain found an ally, Hanover was virtually defenseless. If the French captured it, they could use it as a bargaining tool to obtain a favorable peace settlement in North America.

Newcastle's first choice as an ally was Austria, but his negotiations with Maria Theresa were unsuccessful. He then turned to Russia. On September 30, 1755, the British ambassador in St. Petersburg signed a treaty for the hiring of 55,000 Russian troops. This agreement was based on a misunderstanding. Newcastle intended the Russian troops to protect Hanover from either the French or the Prussians, who were still a French ally. The Russian ruler, Empress Elizabeth, thought that they would be used solely to protect Hanover from her bitter rival, Frederick II of Prussia, whose ambitions along the shores of the Baltic conflicted with her own.

The Russo-British treaty terrified Frederick, who thought that it was directed at him. Newcastle now saw what he thought was a great opportunity. He negotiated a treaty with Prussia, the Convention of Westminster, signed on January 16, 1756. Britain and Prussia agreed to oppose the entry of foreign armies into Germany, although at Frederick's insistence the convention did not cover the parts of the Holy Roman

Empire where German was not the native language. Frederick thereby tried to lure France into attacking the Austrian Netherlands, leaving him the option of remaining neutral or of entering the war if France offered him a sufficient bribe. Meanwhile he delayed extending the alliance with France.[4]

Newcastle and Frederick were too clever for their own good. Empress Elizabeth was outraged at Britain and Prussia. She urged Maria Theresa to join her in attacking Prussia. Maria Theresa agreed but insisted their attack be postponed until 1757 so their armies could be fully mobilized.[5] The Convention of Westminster thus placed Prussia in mortal peril.

The treaty also caused Louis XV to lose interest in renewing the French alliance with Prussia. This placed Hanover in great danger. As he began negotiations with Austria in February 1756, he also was preparing an attack on an important British possession that might cause Britain to begin peace negotiations and avoid expanding the war to Europe. Its success at any rate would end any hope of a quick British victory.

That possession was the Mediterranean island of Minorca, a British colony since its capture from Spain in 1708. It was as valuable as Gibraltar, captured four years earlier. It had a magnificent harbor, was a major base for privateers (privately financed and manned warships used mostly to capture merchant ships), and was defended by a huge fort, St. Philip's Castle. As a French landing force would have to traverse 220 miles of open sea from the great naval base of Toulon, its capture would require deceiving Britain.[6]

During the summer of 1755 France had used British fears of invasion to offset how badly the French navy was outnumbered. At the beginning of 1756, the French government stepped up its efforts to deceive the British into thinking an invasion was imminent. It sent troops to the Atlantic coast of France, thereby raising concern about the squadron being prepared at Toulon. Some, including First Lord of the Admiralty George Anson, feared that it would be sent through the

France Could Have Won the War

Straits of Gibraltar to help escort an invading army across the English Channel. The British government even brought Hanoverian and Hessian troops to England to help defend it.

Anson was a renowned naval hero and a superb administrator, but in 1746 he had shown excessive concern about a French invasion, advocating keeping a large fleet in home waters.[7] He was now so worried about invasion that he was unwilling to send more than ten ships of the line from England to the Mediterranean. His fears were groundless. The French had no transports ready for a Channel crossing, and even if the Toulon squadron had been sent to join the fleet at Brest, the British would still have had enough warships to counter any threat. (On June 1, 1756, the British had eighty-eight ships of the line in service, including fifty-three in home waters, compared with thirty-three French, including eleven in Atlantic ports.)[8] Anson selected Admiral John Byng, a competent ship handler but very cautious squadron commander, to command the ships being sent to protect Minorca.

After a brief stop at Gibraltar, Byng proceeded to Minorca only to find a 15,000-man French army already ashore. He now had thirteen ships of the line, having picked up three that had escaped from Minorca. He immediately sought out the French squadron of a dozen ships of the line that had escorted the army's transports. It was commanded by the marquis de La Galissonière, the former governor general of Canada. The May 20, 1756, Battle of Minorca was indecisive, neither side losing a ship, but Byng's squadron was so damaged that he decided to return to Gibraltar for repairs. Instead of being trapped on the island by a British victory, the French army was free to besiege St. Philip's Castle. Before the British navy could return, the fort and island were captured.

The capture of Minorca gave the French an equivalent for at least Acadia, but the British refused to make peace. English public opinion was angry instead of discouraged. The Newcastle government offered it Byng as a scapegoat, even though Anson, the son-in-law of Newcastle's friend Lord Chancellor Philip Yorke, Earl of Hardwicke, was largely to blame for the debacle. Byng was court-martialed and eventually put to death, but it did not save the Newcastle government. After the North American campaign of 1756 ended unsuccessfully, Newcastle, Hardwicke, and Anson resigned from office. Byng's opponent, La Galissonière, a national hero for winning the French navy's first major triumph in half a century, died of natural causes while en route to be congratulated at the French court.

Three weeks before the Battle of Minorca, the French and Austrians signed a defensive alliance. Because the May 1 Treaty of Versailles would not be operative unless either party was attacked in Europe, most historians have believed that its purpose was to enable France to escape a wider war.[9] This cannot be easily reconciled with the fact that France and Austria immediately thereafter began negotiations for an offensive alliance that would permit France to attack Hanover and Austria to attack Silesia. The resulting Second Treaty of Versailles was signed on May 1, 1757. France promised Austria help against Prussia as well as a subsidy.[10] Britain in turn provided a financial subsidy to Prussia, completing what is called the Diplomatic Revolution. This reversal of allies from the previous war reflects the frequently changing alliance system of the eighteenth century, but it was logical as it paired two nations preparing attacks in central Europe (joined by a third, Russia) against two defenders of the status quo. It was a crucial event in American history as well as European history. Without the Austrian alliance, France might have been forced into an even worse peace than the one it made in 1763, leaving it unable to rebuild its navy or help the United States win its independence. Later, as we shall see, the Austrian alliance helped France keep Europe at peace in 1778 while it went to war against Britain.

Long before the Second Treaty of Versailles was signed,

France Could Have Won the War

hostilities had begun on the European continent.[11] Expecting an imminent attack by Austria, Frederick II opted to strike first. On August 29, 1756, he attacked and soon conquered the electorate of Saxony, a neutral state located between Prussia and Maria Theresa's Kingdom of Bohemia (now the Czech Republic). He then invaded Bohemia but could not win a decisive victory before the onset of winter. During the following spring he tried again, almost capturing Prague, but was forced to retreat to Silesia after the Austrians won the Battle of Kolin on June 18, 1757.

Meanwhile the French began their invasion into Germany by seizing the great Prussian fortress of Wesel on the Rhine (located in a western portion of Prussia) and then occupying it in trust for Austria. After besieging and capturing a nearby smaller Prussian fort, their 100,000-man army marched toward Hanover. To defend it, George had an army half its size, using as its nucleus the Hanoverian and Hessian troops that had served in England the previous year. George also hired troops from several other German principalities. Although this "Army of Observation" had no British troops, George appointed the Duke of Cumberland as its commander. On July 26, 1757, the French defeated it at the Battle of Hastenbeck. The Army of Observation retreated in disorder through Hanover to the port of Stade on the Elbe River. The pursuing French army was exhausted, however, and its commander, Louis-François-Armand Vignerat du Plessis, duc de Richelieu (the captor of Minorca), feared it might disintegrate if it attempted to besiege Stade. On September 8 Cumberland signed the Convention of Kloster Zeven offered to him by Richelieu. His Hanoverian troops were to be interned but not disarmed while the other contingents of the army were free to return to their respective principalities. Cumberland returned to England to face the rage of his father, who repudiated the convention.[12]

The British had nothing else to show for the campaign

of 1757. William Pitt, the secretary of state for the southern department in a new Newcastle government, had expected Loudoun to crush the French and Canadians in a single campaign. He was assigned 11,000 troops (including 6,000 being sent from Ireland) and sixteen ships of the line to capture Louisbourg and then to proceed up the St. Lawrence to Quebec City. Meanwhile 7,500 British and provincial troops were expected to capture the forts on Lake Champlain, opening the way to Montreal. This would enable the British to dictate a favorable peace, although Pitt does not seem as yet to have had plans of retaining Canada.

The British plans were foiled by the genius of Machault and Vaudreuil. When Loudoun's troops from New York rendezvoused at Halifax with the troops from Ireland, Loudoun found his sixteen ships of the line insufficient to support a landing at Louisbourg. Three French squadrons comprising eighteen ships of the line had sailed independently to Louisbourg, arriving within three weeks of each other. (It was Machault's final accomplishment, as he was relieved of office for reasons unrelated to the navy.) Loudoun gave up on his plans and returned to New York,[13] only to discover the offensive against the Lake Champlain forts also had been abandoned. Vaudreuil had sent Montcalm on another spoiling expedition, besieging, capturing, and pillaging Fort William Henry on the southern shore of Lake George.[14]

The outcome of the war now depended on Prussia, whose situation was almost as dire as that of Hanover. Frederick II did crush a ragtag army of French troops and of Imperial troops contributed by the Holy Roman Empire to punish him for his invasion of Saxony. This Battle of Rossbach was a humiliating defeat for France, but it did not save Frederick. While he was in central Germany winning his battle, an Austrian army captured Breslau, the capital of Silesia. Frederick marched against the city, determined to risk everything. The Austrian army unwisely left the fortifications of Breslau.

France Could Have Won the War

Frederick met it in the countryside and, although outnumbered, crushed it in his most brilliant victory, the December 5, 1757, Battle of Leuthen. He soon reentered Breslau, regaining the initiative.[15] He sent one of his best generals, Prince Ferdinand of Brunswick-Wolfenbüttel, to command the Army of Observation, which was renamed His Britannic Majesty's Army in Germany. In early 1758 it drove the French out of Hanover.

The Battle of Leuthen saved both Prussia and Hanover. Had Frederick been defeated and Prussia eliminated from the war, the Army of Observation almost certainly would have disintegrated. This would have left George no chance of regaining Hanover. With nothing to offer except Acadia in exchange for Minorca and Hanover, the British government would have been under great pressure from the king to accept French terms for a settlement of the disputed border between the French and British colonies in North America.

This is somewhat speculative because no one can be sure of the king or the public's reaction to a military disaster of the magnitude of the one suffered in 1940. What seems more predictable is what would have happened had the British accepted peace terms leaving the Upper Country in French and Native American hands. Such a defeat would have left the American colonies desperately dependent on British military and naval support in spite of their anger at Britain's military ineptitude. The Board of Trade's campaign to tighten up colonial administration and end salutary neglect would have had a greatly improved chance of success. Any American drive for independence would have had to wait until after another Franco-British war. The Canadians and Native Americans would have preserved their way of life, at least for a time. All of this was prevented by a battle in what today is Poland, many hundreds of miles from the nearest British soldier.

FIVE

The British Army Could Have Withdrawn
from the American Frontier

T he successful defense of Louisbourg ended in disaster
for the French navy. Although all of its ships returned
safely to France, they brought a terrible epidemic
that killed nearly half of the 17,000 officers and sailors of
the fleet, as well as 5,000 civilians around the ports of Brest
and Rochefort. The navy never recovered. On June 1, 1757, it
had 42 ships of the line in service against 96 British; a year
later it could man only 25 against 104. It made a great effort
to save Louisbourg in 1758, sending 16 ships of the line as
they were ready, but many did not make it. When the British arrived with 23 ships of the line, there were only 6 French
ships of the line in the harbor. The British army, commanded
by General Jeffery Amherst, outnumbered the French garrison by almost four to one. Nevertheless the French resisted
so long that after its surrender on July 26, Amherst did not
have enough time to proceed against Quebec.[1]

Even less successful was the massive army of 6,000 British
regulars, 11,000 provincial troops, and 400 Mohawks sent
to attack the French forts on Lake Champlain. In a humiliating defeat, they failed to breach a makeshift barrier outside
Fort Carillon manned by Montcalm's 3,000 or 3,500 French
regulars that could easily have been destroyed by artillery.
The Mohawks did not participate, preferring to watch from
a nearby hill the spectacle of Europeans killing each other.

After the battle, the British and Americans retreated to Lake George.[2]

The part of the 1758 campaign that was most consequential for subsequent American history was the methodical advance of 1,600 British and 5,000 American troops to Fort Duquesne. This time the advance was entirely through Pennsylvania, with the British commander, General John Forbes, building a road and fortifications along his 100-mile route. When he finally arrived at the onset of winter, he found Fort Duquesne abandoned and destroyed. Facing starvation, its defenders, mostly Native Americans, retreated to the more northern French forts along the Allegheny River.[3]

The most significant part of Forbes's campaign was its aftermath. The Native Americans of the Ohio Country had become disillusioned with the French, largely due to Montcalm's contempt for them. Acting partly for humanitarian reasons, he refused to allow them the booty and captives they expected as their due for their participation in the successful sieges of Oswego and Fort William Henry. Moreover they brought back to their home villages a smallpox epidemic. Thanks largely to pacifist Quaker and Moravian intermediaries, nineteen Indian nations signed a treaty at Easton, Pennsylvania, in October 1758. They agreed to withdraw from the war in exchange for the governor of Pennsylvania's promise that no settlement would be made west of the Allegheny Mountains. This was taken by the Native Americans of the Ohio Country to mean that the British army would depart once Fort Duquesne was destroyed.[4]

There were precedents for such a withdrawal. The French had returned to the north after capturing and destroying Oswego and Fort William Henry. In Europe armies returned to winter quarters once there was no forage for the horses and oxen used to mount cavalry or pull artillery, often abandoning territory they had captured. There were no compelling military reasons for the British to remain at the site of Fort

Duquesne. France's remaining Native American allies, the nations of the far Upper Country and of the mission villages along the St. Lawrence River valley, posed a relatively minor danger; less than 1,000 of them helped defend Quebec City in 1759.[5] The most exposed colonial frontier settlements had been abandoned, and over the last several years a string of forts had been constructed along the Pennsylvania, Maryland, and Virginia frontier. Most important, a daring raiding party of 3,000 provincial troops and boatman recently had crossed Lake Ontario and destroyed Fort Frontenac, the chief supply base for the Ohio Country.[6] Amherst, now commander in chief in America, could have ignored Fort Niagara, the French forts along the Allegheny, Detroit, and the French forts in the Illinois Country (technically part of Louisiana). Lack of supplies would have rendered them almost as harmless as the Japanese islands in the Pacific bypassed during the Second World War.

Instead, the British did not keep the agreement reached at Easton. They not only remained at the site of Fort Duquesne but began building a gigantic new fortification named Fort Pitt. Part of the reason undoubtedly was Amherst's exaggerated fears of Native Americans that slowed his unsuccessful advance on Montreal in 1759 and his successful one in 1760. Mostly, however, the British betrayal of their agreement was a political decision. Land-hungry American colonists and the victory-obsessed British public would have been outraged had the British army pulled back. Pitt, the leader of the British war effort, was undecided about how much of Canada he wished Britain to retain, but he certainly favored keeping his options open.[7] Amherst, who approved the fort, was timid in the face of the enemy, but was unabashedly racist and very ambitious. Broken promises to Native Americans are a near constant in American history. In this case, there was a terrible price to pay for such a horrendous violation. The building of Fort Pitt could not be undone. The British henceforth found it impossible to remove their army from territory claimed by the American colonies and found it difficult to decide the exact purpose of that army. It became a major component of the fatal deterioration of relations between Britain and its colonies.

The capture of Louisbourg removed a major distraction from the British blockade of the Gulf of St. Lawrence. It became increasingly difficult to feed Quebec and Montreal. In spite of enormous efforts by the French government and patriotic merchants like Abraham Gradis of Bordeaux, Canada barely escaped mass starvation.[8] Sending substantial reinforcements would have been pointless even had it been possible. By 1759 the 5,000 remaining French regulars and marines and 10,000 or so Canadian militia faced about 20,000 American troops and 20,000 British troops.[9] Amazingly they delayed Amherst's advance down Lake Champlain long enough to save Montreal and came agonizingly close to defeating General James Wolfe's attack on Quebec City.[10] Even had Quebec escaped, however, it is likely it would have been captured the following year. Fort Niagara also was captured in 1759.

The British failed to attack Louisiana, but in 1760 they captured Montreal, forcing Vaudreuil to surrender all of Canada. The nearly simultaneous arrival at Montreal of armies from Lake Ontario, Lake Champlain, and Quebec is often cited as an example of Amherst's military genius, but his strategy was time-consuming and overly elaborate; each of the three columns could have single-handedly captured the nearly defenseless city and its exhausted and demoralized defenders.

In 1761 the British army occupied French posts like Detroit in the Upper Country and helped defeat a Cherokee uprising in South Carolina. The following year British regulars and American volunteers provided welcome reinforcements for a British army successfully besieging Havana, but suffered terrible losses from disease.[11] Chapter 9 will discuss the end of the war in Europe and the peace negotiations. The British gained all of North America east of the Mississippi River, but the old policy of salutary neglect suffered a fatal blow, in large part due to the problem of what to do with the British troops still in North America.

Initially the British decided to retain 10,000 troops so as to occupy not only Quebec, Montreal, and the heavily populated area along the St. Lawrence River but also Illinois, the Ohio Country, and the Upper Country, inhabited by various Native nations and a number of French traders. Although the stated reason for the decision was the threat posed by French troops supposedly being stationed in the West Indies, the decision actually was based on a number of factors including the desire to avoid alienating politically influential army officers by demobilizing their regiments.[12] The retention of troops in the Upper Country did not ensure peace. Instead it caused a major insurrection by Native Americans outraged at the arrogance, cruelty, and stinginess of General Amherst, who curtailed the provision of hunting supplies they needed for survival.[13] Initially Pontiac and his followers surprised and captured every British post in the Upper Country except for Fort Pitt, Fort Niagara, and Detroit. Lacking artillery they tried unsuccessfully to starve these posts into surrender. They finally agreed because of their shortage of ammunition to a compromise agreement that they hoped would protect their hunting grounds from encroaching American colonists. In October 1763, during Pontiac's rebellion, the British government had issued the Proclamation of 1763, which established a line along the crest of the Allegheny Mountains beyond which colonists were forbidden to settle, land company purchases were outlawed, and licenses for trading with the Native Americans were required.

The British army proved as ineffectual in policing the proclamation line as it had been in enforcing the policies that led to Pontiac's rebellion (and cost Amherst his job). Traders and settlers continued to cross the mountains; the rich lands that became Kentucky especially were flooded with settlers like Daniel Boone. British army officers were at best ambivalent and sometimes hostile to the proclamation, particularly since they depended on white settlers for feeding their garrisons. In 1774 the British tried to resolve the problem by adding the Native American lands north of the Ohio River to the province of Quebec, further outraging the British American colonists.

In contrast the British occupation of Canada proved relatively successful. Although they failed to introduce real self-government and attracted few English-speaking immigrants, the British did respect Catholicism and French civil law. By co-opting rich landowners and the clergy, the British pacified their new Canadian subjects. During the American invasion of 1775–76, most Canadians chose to remain neutral.[14] The problem remained, though, of how British troops could be used in the thirteen colonies south of Canada and Nova Scotia. Some government figures thought that they might be useful in making Americans more compliant subjects of the king. In the late 1760s, the British moved troops into cities of the American seacoast as Americans resisted new British taxes and laws. Two regiments (about 1,000 soldiers), for example, were transferred to New York City in June 1766 in the aftermath of the Stamp Act crisis (discussed in the next chapter) as a warning to Americans. Because British troops were available, the temptation to use them proved irresistible. (Some of the troops came from Halifax, but the garrison was too small a base for a colonial policy based on military coercion, and the British could not strip Quebec and Montreal of their garrisons, so the troops left in America were vital.) The British became involved in a couple of vicious circles. The expense of keeping troops in America created the impetus to impose taxes that required troops to enforce, while the presence of troops produced colonial resistance that necessitated troops to repress.

The main site of military-civilian confrontation was Boston, which had a long tradition of self-government and a large population of sailors, laborers, and artisans experienced in crowd action (such as the annual Pope's Day ritual fighting between the North Boston and South Boston mobs) and distressed by the dislocations of the postwar economy.[15]

With the passage of the Stamp Act, the rioting became political. On August 14, 1765, a mob pillaged the house of stamp agent Andrew Oliver, who was intimidated into resigning his office. Twelve days later, the houses of the controller of customs, the deputy registrar of the vice admiralty court, and Lieutenant Governor Thomas Hutchinson were attacked. Governor Francis Bernard, who fled to Castle William on an island in Boston Harbor, requested troops from Amherst's successor, General Thomas Gage, but then changed his mind. Patriotic rioting occurred until the following February, when rumors of the impending repeal of the Stamp Act calmed the city. The British blamed prominent politicians Samuel Adams and James Otis Jr. for the rioting.

New confrontations began in March 1768, following Parliament's passage of the Townshend Acts. In response Secretary of State for the Colonies Wills Hill, Earl of Hillsborough ordered troops to the city. Two regiments and part of a third (about 1,200 soldiers) from Halifax disembarked at Boston's Long Wharf on October 1, 1768. Two more regiments from Ireland soon arrived. There already was a 50-gun ship, HMS *Romney*, in the harbor serving as a refuge for fleeing customs commissioners.

Although the regiments from Ireland were withdrawn in the summer of 1769, coexistence between the garrison and the 15,000 civilian inhabitants of Boston remained uneasy, particularly since off-duty soldiers competed with civilian workers for scarce jobs. Reciprocal taunting and minor altercations increased the danger of serious bloodshed. Finally on March 5, 1770, a group of civilians pelting a sentry with snowballs provoked eight frightened British soldiers into firing upon the crowd. Five were killed and six wounded in the so-called Boston Massacre. Subsequently one of the two remaining regiments was sent to New York and the other moved to Castle William.[16]

Once again calm returned. The passage of the Tea Act in 1773, however, led to the "Boston Tea Party," which led to another military response to a political program (discussed in chapter 7). As has been said, a revolution is not a tea party, but the American Revolution began with one.

The decision to break the Easton agreement with the nations of the Upper Country did not lead on its own to American independence. It did produce a continuing British military presence in the colonies that interacted dangerously with British attempts to alter traditional relations with the colonists. It eventually produced a mind-set in the British government that political problems could be resolved with military solutions. Since substantial military forces without a clear purpose were available, they could be used to coerce Americans. If the British army had been withdrawn from the colonies and restricted to newly acquired Canada and Florida, dealings with Native Americans could have been left to the individual colonies as they were before the war. The Native Americans would not have fared well, but perhaps not much worse than they fared under ineffective British protection. A major irritant in British-American relations would have been removed, though. The British government would have been forced to consider less confrontational tactics with the American colonies, while Americans who were particularly fearful of standing armies would have been relieved of some of their suspicion of Britain. By constructing Fort Pitt, the British made a permanent military presence in the colonies almost inevitable and the reconstruction of salutary neglect almost impossible.

SIX

The British Government Might Have Learned
a Lesson from the Stamp Act Fiasco

Many Americans were shocked that the victorious peace of 1763 was immediately followed by an era of bad feelings in England toward Americans.[1] They should not have been surprised, as there were important continuities between England's wartime and postwar attitudes. One continuity has been frequently noted by historians, the contempt for America's supposed backwardness and military ineptitude. Another was the widespread taxpayer revolt against high taxes and the large national debt, which were blamed in part on America. As we shall discuss in chapter 9, this revolt began soon after the "miraculous year" of 1759 with its great victories and was largely responsible for Britain's making a peace that left France eager for revenge and still possessed of the means for eventually doing so. This was not unusual. Taxpayer disillusionment also contributed to Britain's making disappointing peaces in 1713, 1748, 1782–83, and 1801–2. What made this revolt unique was the way that the British taxpayer, heretofore chiefly incensed at the expenses of the war in Germany, chose after 1762 to blame America. (The taxpayers who really mattered were the wealthy ones who in large part elected and sometimes sat in the House of Commons and dominated British social, political, and economic life.) This anger was a godsend to those like Halifax and the other members of the Board of Trade who before the war had wanted to end the special treatment of the American colonies.

There were reasons for British resentment. One of the first issues to come up after the war was the blatant way American smugglers had traded with the enemy in the Caribbean.[2] For American merchants and shipowners, this was merely carrying on a tradition that had been going on for decades in war and peace. British soldiers and sailors, in contrast, saw it as aiding the resistance of islands like Martinique and Guadeloupe whose capture cost the lives of British servicemen. In March 1764 Parliament passed the American Duties Act, often called the Sugar Act, the first part of a plan by Prime Minister George Grenville to raise revenue in the American colonies to help offset the cost of maintaining troops there.[3] It also was intended to reduce the smuggling of molasses from foreign colonies in the Caribbean. (Molasses, a by-product of sugar refining, was used in making rum, a huge industry in New England.) The Molasses Act of 1733 had established a heavy import duty on foreign molasses that was designed to benefit the sugar producers of British islands such as Jamaica and Barbados. These islands did not produce enough molasses, though, to supply American distilleries. In response colonial merchants resorted to smuggling from foreign islands like Martinique and Guadeloupe. They were able to bribe British customs officials in America to look the other way. The new act greatly reduced the duty on foreign molasses, but instituted a set of procedures to suppress smuggling. They included requirements that merchants post bond and fill out a cumbersome set of paperwork, measures to root out corruption in the customs service, and, most menacing of all, a provision by which the customs commissioners could move the trials of suspected smugglers to vice admiralty courts in which there were no juries and defendants were presumed guilty unless they could prove their innocence.[4]

The new act was controversial, but its effects were largely limited to merchants. The amount of revenue it was expected to produce was small, and it could be viewed as a measure to regulate trade rather than a tax. Americans were used to such regulations of which the best known were the Navigation Acts that for a century had limited what Americans could produce, where they could send it, and which ships could transport it.

Also limited in its effects was the Currency Act that Parliament passed in April 1764. It prohibited the use of colonial paper money as a legal tender. The New England colonies already were forbidden to do so. The measure was chiefly directed at Virginians who had been using depreciated Virginia currency to pay British creditors.[5] The British government's opposition to colonial currency was generally counterproductive. Given America's need for capital and its widespread unemployment, such a deflationary policy was the opposite of what was needed.

Grenville finally produced widespread American opposition with his most sweeping measure, the Stamp Act of March 1765. It played an important part in the disintegration of American-British relations by opening the question of Parliament's authority to tax the American colonies and by fostering suspicion between Americans and Britons. It was also a symptom of an underlying problem that salutary neglect had allowed to remain hidden. The American colonies were vastly different from Great Britain (and particularly England) with its wide variety of excise taxes on the articles of everyday life and labor, its huge number of excise agents to collect them, its standing army and mighty navy to protect it from its European neighbors, its unreformed Parliament dominated by the rich and well-born, and its huge metropolis of London with its widespread poverty and disease.[6] The American colonies had a more agrarian economy, no large cities, little poverty, and a more egalitarian social

The Stamp Act Fiasco

and political structure (except for those excluded like slaves and Native Americans).

Britons normally took little interest in their American colonies except for business relations. Few members of Parliament or the British government had any firsthand knowledge of the colonies or understanding of the colonists' viewpoint. In contrast Americans took a great interest in Great Britain but had a skewed perspective of it. They tended to view Britain through the eyes of English outsiders like the seventeenth-century opponents of Charles I and James II and the eighteenth-century critics of Robert Walpole. These "commonwealthmen" or followers of the "country party" saw the growing power of the British government as corruption.[7] Given the tensions of British society and the dangers of international relations, the rulers of Britain could not turn back the clock to be more like America, while America was many decades of economic development away from being like England.

Not all of America's fears were imaginary. As the Irish and Scots could testify, the English were arrogant, aggressive, and exploitative. The oligarchy that dominated British social, political, economic, and religious life was hostile to reform and intolerant of reformers. Americans in turn were self-righteous (in spite of their treatment of slaves and Native Americans), acquisitive, and morbidly suspicious of government.[8] The relationship between the two peoples could flourish only on the basis of looking the other way (or letting sleeping dogs lie), the essence of salutary neglect. The Stamp Act challenged the foundations of that relationship.[9]

During the long delay before his introduction of the act in Parliament, Grenville was warned by American colonial agents that the only way of raising revenue that would be acceptable to Americans was asking them to raise it themselves. Americans had responded generously to British requisitions during the war. Pitt had arranged for partial reimbursement to the colonies, but colonial legislatures still had gone into debt by raising troops and supporting the war effort. Grenville disregarded the colonial agents' advice by imposing on the colonies a less sweeping version of Britain's excise taxes to help pay for the troops stationed in America. The stamps Americans were required to purchase had to be embossed on or affixed to items used by most Americans: legal documents, ships' clearance papers, newspapers, liquor licenses, land grants, advertisements in the press, playing cards, dice, and calendars. The sweeping nature of these requirements was an assertion of Parliament's right to tax the colonies.

Such a challenge to the right of the colonies to raise their own revenue assaulted Americans' core belief in self-government and seemed to confirm American fears that the British government was corrupt and power mad. They resisted by making the tax impossible to collect. They intimidated the stamp agents that the British appointed in America to distribute the stamps and prevented the stamps and stamped documents from being landed in America or being removed from storage. The colonies cooperated in a way that was a complete contrast to their rejection of the 1754 Albany Plan for a colonial union for self-defense. Committees of correspondence communicated information among the colonies, and a Stamp Act Congress attended by delegates from nine colonies petitioned for repeal of the act. Merchants and consumers across America acted to boycott British imports and made a widespread effort to manufacture clothing domestically. Long before this widespread resistance took effect, the king removed Grenville from office, largely because of disputes over patronage and because the king detested him personally. His administration was replaced by a weak coalition headed by the young Charles Watson-Wentworth, Marquess of Rockingham.[10] The new first lord of the treasury (and hence unofficial prime minister) was eager to repeal the Stamp Act, but he needed to placate the members of the

The Stamp Act Fiasco

House of Commons who feared for the authority of Parliament (which was also regarded as being threatened by the forceful young king, George III).

Cleverly the Rockingham administration drafted Pennsylvania colonial agent Benjamin Franklin and two dozen other friendly witnesses to testify before the House of Commons. Franklin was particularly useful not only because of his reputation as a scientist, writer, and humanitarian but also because of his prior implicit support of the Stamp Act. Franklin had spent most of the previous nine years in London, the first five of them trying in vain to get Pennsylvania proprietor Thomas Penn to pay his fair share of taxes and loosen his hold over the governors he appointed. For all of his benevolence Franklin could be vengeful when crossed, and his hatred of Penn warped his judgment. After returning to Pennsylvania in 1762, he took up a new crusade, that of replacing Penn's proprietorship with royal government. Already suspicious of the British government, Franklin's constituents failed to reelect him to the Pennsylvania Assembly in 1764. Nonetheless the Assembly reappointed him as colonial agent, and he returned to the London that he like many other resident Americans had come to love. Although he advised against passing the Stamp Act, he underestimated the resistance it would cause and nominated his friend John Hughes as stamp agent for Pennsylvania. During the anti-Stamp Act rioting in Philadelphia, his house was saved by the intervention of his friends and the courage of his wife, who armed herself with a gun to protect it.[11]

Franklin now moved to correct his mistake. In his testimony he affirmed the loyalty of the American colonists and their willingness to respond to requisitions. He also stressed their self-sufficiency and the contribution they had made to British victory in the war. Unfortunately, still out of touch with American opinion, he incorrectly indicated that Americans differentiated between internal taxes designed to raise revenue and external taxes designed to regulate trade. By now Americans were opposed to *all* attempts to raise revenue in America except for that raised by the appropriations of colonial legislatures.[12]

To obtain a majority for repeal, Rockingham had to consent to the simultaneous passage of a Declaratory Act affirming Parliament's authority over the colonies. The repeal of the Stamp Act in March 1766 was met with jubilation in the American colonies. Although still suspicious of the British government and of Parliament, Americans' love of the king was untouched, and most colonists gloried in being not only British but more British than Britons themselves because they remained uncorrupted.[13]

Probably this was Britain's last real chance to save its marriage with America, a marriage Britons regarded paternalistically, but one not yet beyond repair. The repeal of the Stamp Act, however, was an act of the head and of the pocketbook rather than an act of the heart. Britons and Americans had little understanding or sympathy for each other's desires and fears.

A long time of healing was needed to establish some communication. Instead there was only a truce. The Rockingham government lasted only a year before being replaced by one nominally headed by First Lord of the Treasury Augustus Henry Fitzroy, Duke of Grafton.[14] It was expected to be directed by Lord Privy Seal William Pitt, now Earl of Chatham, who was beloved in America. Chatham proved a disaster for relations with the colonies as the informal head of the cabinet. He focused on a quixotic attempt to restore Britain's alliance with Prussia and then, in ill health, largely retired from public life. Real power passed to the young chancellor of the exchequer, Charles Townshend.[15]

Townshend, eager to raise a revenue to pay the salaries of governors and magistrates in America, foolishly accepted Franklin's opinion that external taxes would be acceptable to

The Stamp Act Fiasco

the colonies. He therefore pushed through Parliament a plan to collect import duties on items Americans didn't produce themselves: tea, glass, various kinds of paper, pasteboards, red and white lead, and painter's colors. This outraged the colonists both because it was designed to raise revenue and because it could be used to pay the salaries of colonial governors and magistrates, thus removing the means by which colonial assemblies kept them in check. Moreover, to enforce the duties, a separate bill established an American Board of Customs Commissioners. Again American crowds responded violently, and American merchants and consumers boycotted British goods. Informal committees of inspection developed the more subtle technique of using publicity rather than violence to influence those who refused to honor the boycott. The boycott was not as successful as the one protesting the Stamp Act, and in April 1770 Parliament only partially repealed the duties. They left in place the most important revenue-producing duty, that on tea, although both the Grafton administration and its successor, that of Frederick, Lord North, promised to raise no more taxes to produce revenue. The nearly simultaneous withdrawal of troops from the streets of Boston also reduced tension.

An uneasy truce settled over American-British relations. Lord North was a kinder and more sympathetic person than either Grenville or Townshend, but he was no more knowledgeable about American feelings.[16] He eventually would blunder into a final crisis that would prove beyond his ability to solve.

SEVEN

The British Might Have Avoided War
with the American Colonies

Despite the truce following the repeal of most of the Townshend Duties, British relations with America continued to deteriorate. Many Americans were frightened by rumors that the Anglican (or Episcopal) Church, the established religion in England and several American colonies, planned to name a bishop or bishops for America.[1] Benjamin Franklin, by now the agent in England for several American colonies, created a great scandal by leaking to the American press purloined letters of Governor Thomas Hutchinson of Massachusetts and Lieutenant Governor Andrew Oliver. Franklin apparently wished to blame them rather than the British government for the troubled relations between the Bay Colony and its mother country. When Franklin revealed his involvement, he was publicly humiliated by the Privy Council and stripped of his position as deputy postmaster general for America.[2]

The main irritant was the continuing war of the Board of Customs Commissioners against suspected smugglers. The commissioners had the assistance of the British Royal Navy, already suspect in America for its attempts to dragoon American sailors into serving aboard British warships. The Royal Navy purchased fifteen schooners to help intercept smugglers; in 1772 one of them, the *Gaspee*, ran aground and was burned by Rhode Islanders.[3]

Lord North generally was a voice of conciliation and moderation, but in 1773 he made a disastrous mistake. He decided to assist the British East India Company, which was in financial difficulties and had a surplus of tea. He gave it a rebate on the duties it paid to land its tea in Britain and a monopoly of distribution of the tea in America; able to offer tea at a lower price because of the rebate, it could increase its own revenues and those of the customs service. North did not expect trouble, because some Americans had continued to buy taxed tea (although most Americans drank smuggled tea). Heedless of American sensitivities, however, he decided to use the revenue to pay the salaries of governors and magistrates, one of the objectionable features of the Townshend duties.

The American colonists were stunned by what they regarded as yet another British attack on their freedoms. They treated the tea just as they had Grenville's stamps, refusing to let it be put ashore or, if already ashore, to be distributed. In Charleston, New York, and Philadelphia they were successful, but in Boston Governor Hutchinson planned to offload the tea from three newly arrived ships. On December 14, 1773, 100 or more men disguised as Native Americans dumped 90,000 pounds of tea in the harbor, although they carefully avoided damaging the ships.[4]

Even the mild-mannered North could not ignore this attack on private property. The British government's response surpassed in its scope and severity the worst fears of most Americans and doomed a peaceful resolution of the crisis. It believed that the disorder was specific to Massachusetts (and the work of a small minority within the colony) and decided to make an example of it. In so doing it backed itself into a corner from which it could not escape, ending the last hope of avoiding rebellion or limiting it to New England. With its support, Parliament passed a series of acts commonly known as the Coercive Acts or, in America, the Intolerable Acts. The Boston Port Act closed Boston Harbor to virtually all commerce as of June 15, 1774. The Massachusetts Government Act gave the British power over the upper house of the Massachusetts legislature, town meetings, and even jury selection. An Impartial Administration of Justice Act insulated soldiers and royal officials from being tried in Massachusetts for capital offenses. A new Quartering Act gave the British army the power to commandeer quarters wherever it wished. The Quebec Act, which was not related directly to Massachusetts, turned over the Upper Country to Canada, extending its borders to the Ohio River. This angered not only would-be settlers but also those who feared the Catholicism of the French-speaking inhabitants of Canada. To enforce the laws pertaining to Massachusetts, General Gage, hitherto stationed in New York, was named governor of Massachusetts, arriving in May 1774. The city was heavily garrisoned; by the beginning of 1775 there were nine full regiments and parts of two others, around 4,000 troops. Gage, clearly frightened, wanted even more.

There were reasons for his fears. Many Massachusetts residents considered the Coercive Acts a virtual declaration of war. Local militias began intensive drills, selecting a portion of their members called minutemen for immediate response as well as collecting gunpowder and, where possible, cannon. Gage found himself unable to appoint government officials, such as members of the Massachusetts Council, because his opponents resorted to the usual tactics of noncooperation and intimidation. Government outside of local authorities virtually ceased once Gage dissolved the Massachusetts legislature.

As usual the British underestimated the support for Massachusetts in the other colonies, which were not intimidated. A conference of representatives from every colony but Georgia, the so-called Continental Congress, met in Philadelphia from September 5 to October 26, 1774. This descendant of the Stamp Act Congress approved a Declaration of Rights,

War with the American Colonies

a petition to the king, and addresses to the people of Britain, America, and Canada. It also approved restrictions on trade with Britain to be enforced by local committees of inspection collectively known as the Association. It prohibited consumption of East India Company tea effective immediately, imports from the British Isles effective December 1, and exports to them effective September 10, 1775 (a sop to southern planters dependent on English markets for crops like rice and tobacco). It planned to reconvene on May 10, 1775.[5]

There was overwhelming support in Parliament for the coercive policies of the North government; a Conciliatory Bill introduced in the House of Lords by Chatham on February 1, 1775, was rejected without debate.[6] Behind the scenes, however, there were members of government, particularly the moderate secretary of state for the American colonies, William Legge, Earl of Dartmouth, still willing to seek a compromise solution. Even Lord North tolerated Dartmouth's delay in issuing orders to Gage to seize the leading Massachusetts radicals or the war supplies being stored outside Boston. Between December 1774 and March 1775, Dartmouth conducted informal discussions with Benjamin Franklin, using two sets of intermediaries. The first consisted of the Quaker merchant David Barclay and the Quaker physician John Fothergill, while the other was conducted by the celebrated Admiral Richard Howe, who had fired the opening shots of the Seven Years' War. He was introduced to Franklin by his sister Caroline, who played chess with the American. Franklin had no authority to speak for the Continental Congress and could only guess at what terms it might find acceptable. Howe and the two Quakers had no authority either, although Howe hoped that he and Franklin might be named joint commissioners to conduct formal negotiations.[7]

The best that Franklin could offer was to pay for the tea himself (in hope of being eventually reimbursed). North in turn could suggest nothing better than a plan by which Parliament would name a sum and the Americans could raise it themselves. This would require Americans to acknowledge Parliamentary supremacy, which was unacceptable to them. In early March the discussions sputtered to an end. Later in the month Franklin bid a tearful farewell to his English friends. He sailed for Philadelphia on March 21 or 22, thereby escaping likely arrest for his part in the Hutchinson letters affair.

On February 9, 1775, Parliament declared Massachusetts in rebellion. Orders from Dartmouth to seize the Massachusetts ringleaders already were en route to Gage. He received them on April 14, and on the night of April 18–19 he sent 800 troops to seize Samuel Adams and John Hancock at Lexington and rebel war materiel at Concord. The Americans, with their superb intelligence gathering network and highly experienced messengers like Paul Revere, not only beat the British to Lexington and Concord but also warned surrounding communities of their approach. Hancock and Adams escaped (although Revere was captured), and the British could not find the war supplies hidden near Concord. At Lexington, however, they encountered and fought sixty local militiamen, killing eight of them and wounding another nine.

When the British returned to Concord after their vain search, they had to fight their way over the North Bridge spanning the Concord River. Militia lined the road from Concord back to Boston, fighting from cover as the Native Americans had done against Braddock's army. Without the arrival of reinforcements at Lexington, this army might have met the same fate. It returned to Boston having suffered 270 casualties while inflicting 100 casualties on the several hundred militiamen it had fought.[8]

The various opportunities of avoiding war had been wasted. Now the British had to suppress the revolution they had failed to prevent. The ensuing war would cost the lives of many Americans, Britons, Germans, Frenchmen, Span-

War with the American Colonies

iards, Dutch, and Native Americans; in proportion to population there were more American casualties than any other of its wars except for the Civil War. War breeds war; the War of American Independence was in large part the result of the Seven Years' War, just as the Seven Years' War was engendered by the War of the Austrian Succession. The salutary neglect that had served Britons and Americans so well had been the product of peace between Britons and Frenchmen as well as between Native Americans and colonists. War had destroyed it all.

2

Twelve Ways the British Could Have Overcome American Independence

EIGHT

American Resistance Might Have Been
Fatally Weakened during 1775

Bloodied and demoralized, the British survivors of April 19 rejoined their regiments only to find Boston surrounded by 16,000 militiamen from all over New England. Boston was not in any real danger of capture. The rebels had no warships and few cannon, and the only approach to the city by land was a narrow causeway that the British had fortified. The main problem was feeding both the large garrison and the citizens of Boston who had not fled, although the British did have enough shipping to send food from England and Ireland.[1] Boston, however, was a terrible place from which to mount an offensive. Massachusetts was densely populated, the people were anti-British and angry, and the terrain was difficult. Gage would have preferred his army to be in New York, but even had the transports been available, it would have been disastrous for morale to evacuate Boston. The army remained in Boston, and the government sent three highly regarded generals to bolster Gage's courage: the dashing John Burgoyne, a hero of the British campaign in Portugal in the last war, William Howe, a hero of the Quebec campaign, and Henry Clinton, a veteran staff officer in Ferdinand of Brunswick's army. They sailed on the same ship and arrived in Boston in late May.[2]

The Americans began hostilities with two major assets: the widespread enthusiasm for fighting the British (the so-called *rage militaire*) and the firm control over most American communities exercised by the committees of inspection. They now turned from intimidating consumers of British goods to intimidating supporters of the British government, who came to be called Loyalists.[3] (This control was not universal; in areas where wealthy anti-British "patriots" were viewed as the oppressor, such as the east shore of Maryland, interior North Carolina, or parts of the Hudson River valley, there were pockets of "radical Loyalists.")[4] Almost everything else for making war was missing. The militia units outside Boston were more like the organized mobs that had rioted against stamp distributors than an army.[5] Although adequately fed and clothed for the moment, the American soldiers lacked training, organization, materiel, and such specialists of modern warfare as army engineers. Their commanders were veterans of the provincial regiments of the Seven Years' War like their leader Artemis Ward or inspirational politicians like Dr. Joseph Warren. In spite of its numerical superiority, the American army was very vulnerable to a British attack.

Soon after the arrival of Gage's new subordinates and several thousand reinforcements, the British decided to take the offensive. Their direct target was not the American army but the hills of Dorchester Heights south of Boston from which cannon could imperil the city. They soon changed their objective to the peninsula where the town of Charlestown faced Boston from the north. It also had hills from which cannon could fire on Boston, Bunker Hill, and Breed's Hill. Ward had many sources of information in Boston, and when he received news of the impending British movement, he decided to act first. He chose to send 1,000 of his men to Charlestown first and worry about Dorchester Heights later. His detachment quickly began to fortify the southernmost height, Breed's Hill.

This rash move gave Gage the chance not only to inflict significant casualties but also to terrify the raw militiamen around Boston into deserting their cause. Clinton, the most intelligent of the generals, suggested sending troops across the harbor to the top of the peninsula to pinch off and then capture the entire American detachment. Gage decided to use some 2,200 troops for a frontal assault under the command of Howe. The Americans had no experience in European-style maneuvers, but they were good marksmen and needed to do nothing more complicated than entrenching themselves and repulsing the attackers. On June 17 the British landed near Charlestown, which they burned to prevent snipers from using it. The subsequent battle resembled the ghastly assault on the French lines outside Fort Carillon seventeen years earlier, except that this time the British won when the enemy finally ran out of gunpowder. The British suffered more than 1,000 casualties, a percentage of losses far higher than that in the 1758 battle, while the Americans suffered about 400, including the gallant Dr. Warren.[6]

In terms of numbers it was not a large battle, but it had a lasting impact. Gage was relieved of command and replaced by Howe, who never completely recovered from the trauma of near defeat by the Americans that he had known in the previous war as second line troops not good enough to fight Europeans. Subsequently, he was able to outflank them repeatedly, but he was reluctant to make any more frontal assaults. British morale plummeted while the Americans gained self-confidence. Perhaps most important, the British had lost their only chance of defeating the Americans before they had a real army.

Creating that army was the work of the Continental Congress, which by good fortune reconvened three weeks after the Battles of Lexington and Concord. The second Continental Congress went into permanent session and for want of an alternative became America's supreme executive, legislative, and judicial body.[7] Selected usually by state legislatures, which for the most part had replaced the old colonial legislatures, the new congressional delegates deliberated and voted as a body on important measures, but did much of their work in committee. Blessed with such talented delegates as Benjamin Franklin and John Adams, Congress had the difficult task of improvising a national political and military structure without provoking the opposition of the thirteen component states. It quickly nationalized the improvised army of New Englanders so as to attract recruits from the rest of America, renaming it the Continental army. Fortunately the most militarily experienced of the delegates, former colonel of the Virginia Provincial Regiment George Washington, was from the south. He was unanimously elected commander of the Continental army and soon left for Cambridge, Massachusetts, headquarters of the troops besieging Boston.[8] His courage, wisdom, and adaptability would make him the single most important contributor to American independence.

He arrived on July 2 to find not a professional army in the making but a large-scale version of the provincial regiment he had once commanded: a group of recent civilians on short-term enlistments with little respect for hierarchy and little taste for military discipline. At least Congress provided him with some good subordinate generals, including two former mid-level British army officers, Horatio Gates and Charles Lee, and a brilliant young former militia officer, Nathanael Greene. He also received other help from Congress, including a visit from a congressional committee including the former commander of the Pennsylvania Provincial Regiment, Benjamin Franklin. It drafted not only a useful set of disciplinary regulations but also the lyrics for a drinking song making fun of British regular soldiers, written of course by Franklin.[9]

Nonetheless Washington faced a multitude of problems including the progressive shrinking of the size of his army until by the end of the year its numerical advantage over the British garrison of Boston had disappeared. The most frightening problem was the acute shortage of gunpowder. America did not have enough saltpeter, one of its ingredients, to

American Resistance in 1775

be self-sufficient, and not enough was brought in from the Caribbean islands and Europe. Washington disguised the shortage, but had the British attacked, they could have decimated his army and threatened America's de facto independence. The British government, as we shall see, was making efforts to collect a huge army for 1776 and shift the war to New York, so their existing army was content to wait out the winter in Boston.

Instead, the fighting shifted elsewhere. Congress was eager to drive the British from Canada and add it to their union. It disregarded the effect of American prejudice against Catholicism on the still mostly French-speaking province and prepared a two-pronged offensive. One column drawn from a separate army under Washington's authority but not his personal command left upstate New York for Montreal. It was under the command of General Richard Montgomery, another British army veteran. A second column left for Quebec City from Maine, then a part of Massachusetts. It was commanded by Benedict Arnold, a dynamic young officer who at the beginning of hostilities had helped Ethan Allen capture Fort Ticonderoga, the successor to Fort Carillon. The once-mighty fort had fallen into disrepair and had only a few dozen defenders, but it was well supplied with cannon that eventually proved invaluable to the Continental army. Despite Arnold's epic march through the wilderness and Montgomery's capture of Montreal, the invasion ultimately failed. A joint attack on Quebec City on December 31, 1775, was beaten back. Montgomery was killed and Arnold wounded. During the following spring, the American army, crippled by smallpox, was driven out of Canada.

Another important theater of war was Massachusetts Bay and the other waters off Massachusetts. On his own authority Washington outfitted a small fleet of lightly armed schooners to intercept the ships bringing supplies from England. The biggest prize was the *Nancy* carrying all the equipment needed for an army's worth of cannon.[10] Washington eventually got the cannon to go with the equipment. His amateur but energetic chief of artillery, Colonel Henry Knox, brought sixty of them during the winter by sled from Ticonderoga, hastening the liberation of Boston in April 1776.

The success of Washington's squadron and the lobbying of Massachusetts delegate John Adams persuaded Congress to approve a Continental navy to go with the Continental army. Its first ships were converted merchant ships, but Congress's plans kept expanding, partly because spreading shipbuilding among the states would broaden support for the war. The new ships authorized by Congress mostly were frigates of 24 to 36 cannon. Building more than a dozen of them stretched Congress's financial resources as well as the supply of sailors, so the new navy made only a small contribution to the war effort.[11]

By the end of 1775, it was clear that America would have great difficulty creating on its own an army capable of standing up to the British. Washington's army opposite Boston had survived since Bunker Hill more due to British deficiencies in troops and confidence than by its own efforts. Everything was in short supply: gunpowder, European-style muskets which unlike rifles could carry a bayonet, military supplies of all sorts, and military specialists like artillerymen and engineers. Congress created a Secret Committee to purchase supplies and a Committee of Secret Correspondence to communicate with American sympathizers abroad, but little had happened as yet when in December the latter committee had a surprise visitor.

He was an unassuming young man from the French West Indies named Julien-Alexandre Achard de Bonvouloir et Loyauté, who had visited America previously and had met members of the First Continental Congress. When Franklin and the other members of the Committee of Secret Correspondence met with him in Carpenters' Hall, Philadelphia, they

American Resistance in 1775

realized he was more important than he was willing to admit. He could not say so, but he was a secret representative of none other than Charles Gravier, comte de Vergennes, the foreign minister of France, the country that could best help America. During his three meetings with the committee, Bonvouloir explained that even though he was only a private citizen, he could convey a message about the needs of Congress. The committee responded that Congress desired information about France's intentions (a matter too delicate for Bonvouloir to answer), two or more good engineers, and the right to purchase guns and other munitions directly from France. (Bonvouloir recommended that they send ships to try, but not always to the same port.) Bonvouloir soon reported to the French ambassador in London, Vergennes's intermediary, about his conversations before he returned to obscurity.[12]

Bonvouloir's brief visit had important consequences both in America and in France. Before discussing them I must first explain the background to Bonvouloir's mission. Only a dozen years earlier, Britain had inflicted on France what appeared to be a crushing defeat. In the intervening years France had suffered a terrible setback in European affairs that further tarnished its reputation. A new peace-loving young king recently had assumed the French throne. How would it be possible for France to risk war by assisting the American rebels?

To answer these questions I must interrupt the flow of the narrative and return to the Seven Years' War. I will look at it in an unfamiliar way, seeing the French not as the allies of the Native Americans attacking frontier settlements but as the future saviors of the United States. If France had not improved its fortunes during the latter years of the Seven Year' War, it would not have been able to come to America's assistance during the American Revolution. I will begin with 1759, the nadir of France's fortunes.

NINE

The Seven Years' War Could Have
Permanently Weakened the French Navy

A s 1759 came to an end, King Louis XV faced a terrible combination of public and private disasters. A promising offensive in Germany was turned back at the Battle of Minden near the border of the Electorate of Hanover. An elaborate plan to invade England or Scotland devised by the new French foreign minister, Etienne-François, duc de Choiseul, ended with the humiliating defeat of a French fleet at the Battle of Quiberon, six ships of the line being captured or destroyed. The navy's chief bankers declared bankruptcy, the army's bankers narrowly escaped the same fate, and the French government had to suspend payment of its debts. Following the example set by Louis XIV in 1709, the king sent his dining services to be melted into coins. (Wealthy Frenchmen followed his example by contributing money to replace the ships of the line lost at Quiberon.) Undoubtedly worst of all for the sentimental king was a terrible personal tragedy, the death from smallpox of his beloved eldest daughter, duchesse Marie-Louise-Elizabeth of Parma, whom he called Babette. At the time of her death she was visiting Versailles to arrange the marriage of her daughter to the eldest son of Empress Maria Theresa.

Had Louis's courage failed, France might have been forced into a disastrous peace. Somehow the terrible blows awakened the pride and stiffened the resolve of the hitherto weak and indecisive king. He decided to strengthen France's efforts in Germany in order to salvage an honorable peace. Even Choiseul, renowned for his bravery in battle, came to admire the king's henceforth unshakable courage.[1]

This courage would be all the more needed when the capture of Montreal and surrender of Canada in 1760 transformed Britain's war objectives. In the early spring of 1761 Pitt, hitherto undecided about whether Britain should retain Canada, decided that when peace was negotiated, Britain should keep it. Moreover, he insisted that Britain should also refuse to share the Newfoundland and St. Lawrence fisheries with France by denying French fishermen facilities to dry the cod they had caught. He threatened to resign if the cabinet opposed him.[2]

The implications of this objective were breathtaking. Sailors trained in the rough waters of the fisheries formed a quarter of the crews of the French navy during wartime and were among the best in the service. Without them the French navy could never hope to challenge the British navy. The British government could pursue without fear of foreign interference its plans to change Britain's relationship with its American colonies.

Both governments realized what was at stake. Choiseul called the fisheries his obsession (*folie*). Pitt in turn claimed that he would rather lose his right arm than permit France access to the fisheries; after the war was over, he bemoaned the loss of an opportunity to impose a peace from which it would have taken France a century to recover.[3] His plans were foiled because France now had a bargaining chip, a conquest in Germany made in 1760 but then almost lost.

In spite of the defeat at Minden, the French army in Germany had begun to improve, largely due to the efforts of Charles-Louis-Auguste Fouquet, duc de Belle-Isle, a celebrated soldier appointed war minister in March 1758. All that was needed was a capable army commander, and in 1760

Louis found one, Victor-François, duc de Broglie. To pay for this army, Louis virtually demobilized the French navy, sending only 14 ships of the line to sea against 111 British. Thus France was able to provide 150,000 men for the army in Germany to fight Ferdinand of Brunswick's 80,000-man Army of His Britannic Majesty. Although Broglie was not able to reoccupy Hanover, he was able on July 31, 1760, to capture Kassel, the capital of Hesse-Kassel, one of the chief sources of troops for Ferdinand's army.

When Ferdinand failed to recapture the city, he ordered one of the boldest moves of the war. He sent his nephew Karl Wilhelm Ferdinand, Hereditary Prince of Brunswick-Wolfenbüttel, with 24,000 British and German soldiers to the Rhine to attack the great fortress of Wesel, garrisoned by only 1,500 French troops. Fortunately for France, some 12,000 reinforcements for Broglie's army were at nearby Cologne when the hereditary prince approached Wesel. Their commander, Belle-Isle's nephew General Charles-Eugène-Gabriel de La Croix, marquis de Castries, rushed to the rescue. On the night on October 15–16, 1760, he camped near the convent of Kloster Kamp, ten miles from Wesel. The hereditary prince launched a night attack on Castries's army, capturing his subordinate, General Philippe-Henri, marquis de Ségur, but the alarm was given. Thanks largely to Castries's best regimental commander, Jean-Baptiste-Donatien de Vimeur, comte de Rochambeau, the attack was repulsed. The hereditary prince abandoned his plans to capture Wesel and returned to his uncle.

The narrow French victory at Kloster Kamp averted a disaster. One of the most astute statesmen in Europe, Spanish foreign minister Ricardo Wall, believed that the loss of Wesel, their gateway to northern Germany, would have forced the French to abandon Kassel and withdraw across the Rhine.[4]

Had these things happened, France would have lost an equivalent for the fisheries and put Louis under pressure to

The French Navy

make whatever peace he could. Without the fisheries, the French navy would not have been in a position to fight the British during the American Revolution, let alone contribute to the victory of Yorktown in 1781, which saved Washington's army from starvation and the Continental Congress from bankruptcy.

There are other connections between Kloster Kamp and Yorktown. Not only was Rochambeau commander of the French contingent at Yorktown, but the French naval minister in 1781 was Castries and the army minister was Ségur!

Although the British effort in Germany was costing astronomical sums and helping to turn taxpayers against the war, peace negotiations in 1761 failed, largely due to Pitt's opposition to any concessions on the fisheries. Instead France reached agreement with Spain on a new alliance and the eventual entrance of Spain into the war. Pitt, knowing of the alliance, urged the cabinet to approve a surprise attack on the Spanish treasure fleet returning from the Western Hemisphere. Anson, again overly cautious, feared a war against both the French navy and the Spanish navy. He and other members of the cabinet were tired of Pitt's intransigence and bullying and refused their consent. Pitt resigned his office in disgust. A few months later, Spain went to war against Britain.[5]

On the surface, the war with Spain was a great success for Britain, which captured Havana and Manila. Spain, however, had been a major trading partner of Britain's, and the war helped cause a 13 percent drop in British exports and a rise in unemployment.[6] Moreover the British had to send troops to Lisbon to protect Portugal from a Spanish invasion.[7] It was one war too many for the taxpayers to bear. Parliament was willing to fund the war in Germany for a final year, but it stopped funding Britain's subsidy to Prussia, which found a new ally in Russia after Frederick's archenemy, Empress Elizabeth, died.

Peace negotiations with France resumed in 1762. John

Stuart, Earl of Bute, the former tutor of George III (who succeeded his grandfather in late 1760), replaced Newcastle as first lord of the treasury in May 1762. Bute was so anxious to end the unpopular war that he began leaking to Choiseul Britain's bottom line in the negotiations.[8]

The fisheries were no longer the chief obstacle. Bute eventually permitted the French not only places to dry their cod but even possession of the small islands of St. Pierre and Miquelon as refuges for their fishing boats. The return of the Caribbean islands captured from France was a problem, but the main dispute was not about the rich sugar islands of Guadeloupe and Martinique, captured in 1759 and 1762, respectively. If the British kept one or both of them, it would have been unwelcome competition for British sugar-producing islands like Jamaica. Even more important, France would never have agreed to Britain's keeping them because trade with them also was vital to training sailors for the French navy. Instead the dispute was over the former neutral islands that produced little or no sugar but were strategically important. France agreed to Britain's keeping Grenada, St. Vincent, Tobago, and Dominica, but obtained St. Lucia, near Martinique.

Another key issue was North America. Choiseul had given up on Canada, which was expensive and indefensible; it was clear, too, that Britain would not return it. The problem was Louisiana, which the British wished to restrict to west of the Mississippi River. France wished a Native American buffer state or at least a corridor several miles wide east of the river. Eventually the French gave way, but convinced the British to let them keep the city of New Orleans. Choiseul argued that the city was not on the east bank of the river but on an island between two channels of the river, the easternmost of which flowed into Lake Pontchartrain. Perhaps out of ignorance of geography, the British eventually conceded this absurd claim, although this left both banks of the lower

Mississippi in foreign hands and hence liable to be closed to boats on the river. (Two decades later this would bedevil the United States.) The British also returned most of the French trading posts in India it had captured, but the British East India Company retained its rights in captured Bengal, giving it an insurmountable lead in the contest for supremacy in the subcontinent.[9]

The main obstacle to peace now was King Charles III of Spain, Louis XV's distant cousin, who had obtained none of his objectives. Louis was unwilling to make peace without him. The impasse was broken at the beginning of October when news arrived of the British capture of Havana. Bute leaked to Choiseul the cabinet's decision that Britain would accept Puerto Rico or Florida in exchange for Havana. Louis cleverly tied Charles's hands by secretly offering Spain New Orleans and the portion of Louisiana west of the Mississippi in compensation for Spain's war losses. (France had come to realize the limited economic value of western Louisiana.)[10] Charles reluctantly agreed to give up West and East Florida because western Louisiana would at least provide a buffer for Mexico. News of its impending transfer was kept secret until long after peace was signed.

The negotiators managed to reach agreement just before news arrived that Ferdinand's long siege of Kassel finally had been successful. On November 3, 1762, a preliminary peace agreement was signed by representatives of Britain, France, and Spain at the chateau of Fontainebleau, south of Paris. On the same day the Spanish representative secretly agreed to Spanish acceptance of western Louisiana. King Louis XV expressed relief that the peace was not as bad as might have been expected.[11] A final peace treaty with a few minor changes was signed on February 10, 1763, and five days later Austria made peace with Prussia on the basis of restoring things to their prewar condition.[12] Russia and Sweden had already made peace with Prussia on the same condition. By his tenacity and courage Louis had saved France's ability to rebuild its navy.

All wars are cruel and dangerous. Most are enormously expensive in money and lives. Some, however, like World War II or the American Civil War, are unavoidable. The Seven Years' War was not one of them. It was unnecessary and ended more or less badly for every country and people involved, even those who appeared to be victorious. Many historians have treated the war like an athletic contest with a winning team (Great Britain and its colonies as well as Prussia) and a losing team (France, its American colonies, Native Americans, Austria, Sweden, and Russia). It is more appropriate to treat it like a train wreck. Many people involved in it were valiant, but its result was uniform disaster. It is more useful to study its causes and consequences than to ask who won; nobody really did when its human and financial costs are counted.

It is easy to see the costs for those who wagered war and lost. Particularly poignant are the damages suffered by those who wished to remain neutral: Acadia, Saxony, Hanover, Portugal, and Poland (overrun by Russian troops en route to fighting the Prussians). They received no compensation for their suffering. Even the supposed winners paid a heavy price. Prussia won in terms of retaining Silesia, but it suffered perhaps 400,000 deaths (a tenth of its population), temporary occupation, and economic dislocation. It would take fifty years for the Prussian army to regain its effectiveness.[13]

The other supposed victors in the war were Great Britain and its American colonists. (Britain's Native American allies such as the Mohawks fared little better than did Britain's Native American enemies, although their distance from the frontier bought the Mohawks and other Iroquois a brief grace period.)[14] The war did permit the colonists to advance their frontier far into Native American hunting grounds, but it also led to decades of war with the Native Americans who lived and hunted there. It also helped lead to a terrible war of separation from the colonists' mother country.

The war also undermined Britain's position in the European balance of power for much the same reasons as it undermined Britain's relationship with the colonists: it fostered a combination of arrogance stemming from British victory and insecurity because of the government's debt. Eventually the British spurned an excellent means of suppressing the American rebellion by rejecting a French overture for better relations that might have given Britain a free hand in America.

TEN

The British Might Have Accepted
France's Pleas for Better Relations

Breaking the alliance with Prussia in 1762 to save expenses left Britain without a major ally in Europe. The various factions competing in Parliament had conflicting ideas of where to find a postwar ally. Some like Pitt favored restoring the Prussian alliance, others favored an Austrian alliance, while still others favored an alliance with Russia, whose large army had fought valiantly against Prussia. The best bet in 1763 was Russia. The previous year had seen it shift from being a bitter enemy of Prussia to being an ally of Prussia under Empress Elizabeth's successor, Emperor Peter III, then to being neutral under Peter's widow, Empress Catherine II. (In July Catherine had supported a coup that overthrew her husband and soon after had winked at his murder.)[1] Her alliance could have been purchased early in her reign by offering Russia a subsidy, but Britain refused to give a subsidy during peacetime, given past failures of such subsidies and the size of the national debt.[2] The opportunity passed when Catherine's confidence rose. She now demanded help against her enemy, the Turks of the Ottoman Empire who blocked Russia's drive to reach the Black Sea. Because Austria was still allied with France and because Prussia was committed to making a Russian alliance without a third party, Britain entered what is called, rather dubiously, "splendid isolation."[3]

Britain was able to defend itself without an ally because Choiseul, who was anxious for revenge, did not have the necessary resources to attack it, even with Spanish assistance. During the period immediately after the war, the French navy depended on the money contributed by the French public to build ships of the line to replace those lost at Quiberon and elsewhere. Choiseul had borrowed from the money to conduct the mostly unsuccessful naval campaign of 1762 (although a small squadron did capture and briefly hold St. John's, Newfoundland). Only two ships of the line were launched by war's end, but over the next four years the French navy launched fifteen more donated ships, purchased another, and rebuilt three more. It was not enough. During the same period Spain launched only eight ships of the line. Choiseul postponed indefinitely his war of revenge. He expected the Americans eventually to revolt, but he told Louis that he did not expect that they would live long enough to see it. He was half correct; the king died of smallpox in 1774. By that year the navy had sixty ships of the line, almost all sitting in port unmanned. This was about a dozen more than it had at the beginning of 1763 and roughly half the number possessed by the British navy. On the other hand, the interwar period was a boom time for colonial trade and fishing. When the necessary ships finally were built or repaired in 1776–78, there were sailors to man them.[4]

The main reason that Choiseul abandoned his plans for attacking Britain, however, was the rising threat from Russia. This was part of the shift of power from France and Britain to the great eastern powers, Russia, Prussia, and Austria.[5] In 1766 Choiseul left his post as naval minister to return to the foreign ministry. Empress Catherine II had demonstrated her power by arranging the election of one of her former lovers, Stanislas Poniatowski, to the Polish throne when the reigning king of Poland died soon after the end of the war. The French Foreign Ministry took few steps to oppose his election. Resistance against the Russians was organized surreptitiously by a secret diplomatic service run by Louis XV over the past twenty years, the "Secret du Roi." This body was first established to elect a French prince to the Polish throne and had gradually evolved into an anti-Russian organization. It was also used for other clandestine purposes such as mapping landing sites along the English coast.[6] It attracted an odd mixture of agents ranging from quacks to ambassadors playing a double role. To avoid detection, it even recruited the brilliant head of the Paris police and chief administrator of the city of Paris, Antoine-Raymond-Gualbert-Gabriel de Sartine. One of its most dedicated members was the French ambassador in Constantinople, the comte de Vergennes, a nobleman who was purged from his post for the social sin of marrying a commoner.[7]

In 1768 the largely Roman Catholic Poles revolted against Catherine's pretensions to represent those in Poland practicing the Russian Orthodox faith. The rebels stood little chance, being wedged between Russia and its ally Prussia, which claimed to represent the Protestants of Poland. Russian troops occupied the country. With Choiseul's encouragement, the Turks entered the struggle against Russia, and a full-scale war ensued.

The British took little interest in the war except for assisting a Russian fleet sailing from the Baltic to the Mediterranean to fight the Turks.[8] They instead spent the decade after the end of the Seven Years' War engaged in a series of tests of strength with France and Spain over mostly trivial issues. The French did score an important victory, though, by purchasing Corsica from Genoa with only minor British opposition.[9] The most serious confrontation took place at the end of the 1760s. The British planted an outpost on an uninhabited island in the Falkland Islands, which the Spaniards discovered and expelled. The British public was prepared for war, but North arranged a peaceful solution. Spain restored the

British garrison under a secret promise from North that Britain would silently withdraw it once the public lost interest.[10] (This resembled President Kennedy's promise to silently withdraw American missiles from Turkey in exchange for Russia's withdrawing its missiles from Cuba during the 1962 Cuban missile crisis.) Choiseul supported Louis's policy of nonintervention, but when in late 1770 his support appeared to be weakening, Louis dismissed him from office.

After a six-month period with an unqualified interim foreign minister, Louis appointed to the post Choiseul's bitter enemy, Emmanuel-Armand de Vignerod du Plessis de Richelieu, duc d'Aiguillon, a supporter of the king in his ongoing dispute with the Parlements, the French higher law courts.[11] D'Aiguillon was ignored by the powers of eastern Europe as the Russo-Turkish war entered a crisis. Russian gains from the Turks threatened to be so large as to endanger the balance of power and possibly provoke a war with Austria. Frederick II devised a solution to avoid further hostilities by persuading Catherine to spare the Turks from dismemberment of the Ottoman Empire. Instead, Russia, Prussia, and Austria each took a chunk of territory from the helpless Poles, who lost 29 percent of their land and 35 percent of their population.[12] This violation of the remaining norms of diplomatic practice was a disaster for French foreign policy, even worse than its defeat in the Seven Years' War. Vergennes, now French ambassador in Sweden after d'Aiguillon rescued him from his disgrace, anguished, "If force is a right, if convenience is a title, what henceforth will be the security of states?"[13] The British government in contrast paid little attention to the partition.

The partition of Poland threatened to unravel France's set of informal alliances in eastern Europe, the "barrier of the east." Sweden, whose monarch had almost as little power as the elected kings of Poland, seemed likely to be next. Vergennes helped finance a 1772 bloodless coup d'état by which Gustavus III seized power from the Swedish Diet and then signed an alliance with France. The Russians assembled troops and threatened war with Sweden, while France turned to what seemed its only hope, the British government.[14] D'Aiguillon sent a secret agent to London to discuss cooperation and better relations. It is unclear which members of the British government were involved, but a leading figure was Northern Secretary of State Henry Nassau de Zuylenstein, earl of Rochford, one of the most experienced of a rather lackluster group of interwar secretaries of state. Even George III showed interest in better relations, but the fear of public opinion and suspicion of France caused the British to break off discussions. The British government then added insult to injury. The French sought to show support for Sweden by outfitting a squadron at Toulon to menace the Russian Mediterranean fleet. The British threatened war against the French if they continued, and France backed down. Domestic problems in Russia saved Sweden from attack, and the long Russo-Turkish war ended in 1774, but irreparable damage had been done to Franco-British relations.

The timing of the crisis over the Toulon squadron is revealing. It coincided exactly with North's introduction of the Tea Act. This demonstrates that North did not realize that the Tea Act would produce a crisis in America: why would he simultaneously gravely insult the country most likely to come to the colonists' aid if he thought there was danger of a rebellion? The rejection of France's overtures for better relations made such assistance more likely. It became even more likely when Louis XV, engaged in a power struggle with the Parlements and hence uninterested in foreign involvements, died in May 1774. The new king, Louis's young grandson, was anxious to be popular and undid his grandfather's attempts to curb judicial opposition. Louis XVI also abolished the Secret du Roi. He was peace loving and cautious like his grandfather in his later years, but he made a fatal mistake. On the advice of his aged informal first minister, Jean-Frédéric Phé-

The Pleas for Better Relations

lypeaux, comte de Maurepas, he chose as his foreign minister the supposedly equally cautious comte de Vergennes.

Albert Sorel, one of the greatest of all diplomatic historians, once described the selection of Vergennes as the accession to power and stunning revenge of the Secret du Roi.[15]
Vergennes took less interest in colonies than did Choiseul
and did not hate the English; he was impressed by their effi-
ciency at raising money for war and later expressed his regret
that the rivalry between Britain and France had permitted
the rise of Russia.[16] He knew, however, of the help that the
British had given the Russian fleet and had seen at first hand
the cooperation of the British and Russian ambassadors in
Stockholm as well as the unfolding of the Swedish crisis. Like
other members of the Secret du Roi, he saw Russia as the chief
threat to France and viewed Britain as Russia's enabler. The
American Revolution gave him what he saw as an opportunity to indirectly weaken Russia by depriving Britain of its
partial monopoly of American trade.

He was assisted at the Foreign Ministry by two chief under-
secretaries of state (each called a *premier commis*), the brothers Conrad-Alexandre and Joseph-Mathias Gérard. They
were law experts from Alsace who, although not technically
members of the Secret du Roi, had been its fellow travelers.
Conrad-Alexandre had undertaken a secret mission to meet
with Jan Klemens Branicki, head of the Polish underground.
Joseph-Mathias was blamed by Frederick II for organizing
Danzig's opposition to being absorbed by Prussia and had
translated into French an English pamphlet against the Polish partition.[17] Each played an important role in the diplomacy of the War of American Independence.

France took a great interest in America after hostilities
began. American ships began arriving in France and the
French West Indies in search of gunpowder. French officials
who might have turned them back if relations with Britain had
been better looked the other way. Private enterprise proved

insufficient to arm the Continental army and save the revolution. The French ambassador at the British court recommended sending the chevalier de Bonvouloir to contact the Americans. Vergennes agreed. Bonvouloir's instructions were to report on the American rebellion and to assure the Americans that France had no designs on Canada and would welcome American ships.[18] The arrival at the French court of his report about his meetings with the Committee of Secret Correspondence sparked a debate in Louis XVI's council of state with enormous consequences for both France and America.

ELEVEN

King Louis XVI Could Have Refused to Arm the Americans

V ergennes received Bonvouloir's report on February 27, 1776. Two weeks later he presented a memoir to a select committee of the king's council of state, consisting of the naval minister, army minister, and controller general (finance minister). Knowing that Louis XVI was dedicated to domestic reform and opposed to war, Vergennes disingenuously presented intervention in the American rebellion not as a step toward war but as a precaution against America making peace with Britain and joining in an attack on the French West Indies. If the rebellion lasted another year, France would have time to bolster the defenses of its Caribbean colonies. He recommended that France and Spain secretly provide arms to the Americans while assuring Britain of their good intentions. He asked the other members of the committee to prepare written responses.

Vergennes's fears for the French West Indies probably were bogus. He had intelligence from Britain that it had neither the immediate capacity nor the desire for war with France. The French West Indies recently had been reinforced, and more troops were not sent until the autumn of 1777. Moreover, until the summer of 1777, the French navy did not prepare for immediate hostilities.[1]

The responses were ready by early April. Vergennes presented a follow-up memoir, "Reflections on the current situation of the British colonies . . . ," prepared by his brilliant undersecretary, Joseph-Mathias Gérard. It was more frank than the previous memoir. It argued that even if France did nothing, war with Britain was inevitable, and that if the Americans were successful, Britain's position in the balance of power would be weakened. The army and navy ministers supported intervention, but Controller General Anne-Robert-Jacques Turgot's memoir recommended a cautious policy of letting the Americans purchase arms from France rather than having the king provide them. Equally important, he demolished the arguments presented in the "Reflections." He stressed that the weakness of the king's finances presented the chief danger to France and argued that France would benefit from a British victory over the rebels because holding the American colonies by force would be a continual drain on British resources. He even argued that France's colonies cost more than they were worth.

Ironically, Turgot was a great admirer of Benjamin Franklin, but his chief concern was reforming the monarchy's finances. On most of his points he was right, and Vergennes, a believer in the old ideas of mercantilism, was wrong. Britain was not weakened by the loss of its partial monopoly of American trade; soon after the end of the war, it enjoyed greater trade with America than ever, thanks to its knowledge of American tastes and its enormous capital resources.[2] In its hopeless quest to weaken Britain, the French government spent itself into eventual bankruptcy and revolution. Louis himself would perish under the guillotine.

The king decided in favor of Vergennes. On May 2 he authorized a subsidy of 1 million livres (about £40,000 or some $5 to $10 million in contemporary money) for the Americans to purchase arms; Spain provided a similar subsidy. Surplus arms and other war supplies would be supplied at cost to a dummy commercial house named Roderique Hortalez and Company in order to shield the government from having to deal directly with the Americans. The company was to be headed by the playwright Pierre-Augustin Caron de Beaumarchais, who had been used in the past by Sartine and Vergennes to pay off a member of the Secret du Roi in England who was blackmailing Louis XV. The name of the company reflected Beaumarchais's interest in things Spanish as evidenced by his recent play, *The Barber of Seville*.[3] Ten days later the king removed Turgot from office. Turgot had angered French public opinion by his policy of free trade of grain within France, which had disrupted the provisioning of Paris.

A key element in the new program was the French navy. It was now under the direction of Vergennes's former colleague Sartine. The royal council of state, notorious for its infighting, now enjoyed a rare stability under the political alliance of Vergennes, Sartine, and unofficial chief minister Maurepas, himself a former naval minister. On April 22 the king authorized Naval and Colonial Minister Sartine to send a few small ships to the West Indies, to hold in readiness a dozen ships of the line at Brest and eight at Toulon in case of a British blockade, to complete ship overhauls in process and those deemed necessary, and to fill magazines and arsenals.

Like Vergennes, Sartine took advantage of the idealistic, inexperienced, and naïve young king. He began a massive program of repairing the navy's aging ships of the line and constructing new ones, spending far more money than the king authorized. Only twenty-four of the navy's sixty ships of the line were in condition for service when Sartine took over in August 1774, and another four were in construction. During 1776 and 1777, the navy overhauled twenty-three ships of the line and launched five others. When hostilities with Britain began in the summer of 1778, the navy was able to put fifty-two ships of the line in service compared with sixty-six British ships of the line in service, the closest approach to parity in seventy years. The American war was the only war of the eighteenth and early nineteenth century in which the French navy had had adequate time to prepare its ships and dockyards; not coincidentally, it was the only war that the French navy won.[4]

The timing of France's involvement in the American Revolution was dictated more by the pace of naval reconstruction than by what was happening in America. Throughout the ups and downs of the fighting in America, the rebuilding of the navy continued, and as it approached its conclusion, the French made an alliance with the United States and prepared to enter the hostilities. All that could have interrupted the rebuilding was the destruction of the Continental army or the outbreak of a premature British war with France. By the time the rebuilding was complete, the American cause was stalemated so that French direct intervention was both necessary and possible.

Bonvouloir's visit also had a major impact on the Continental Congress. Until his arrival, Congress was reluctant to take any irreversible steps to claim the independence that it was in fact exercising. On July 8, 1775, Congress had signed the so-called Olive Branch Petition and sent it to England with a member of the Penn family on the off-chance it would move George III. He ignored it. Even those like Franklin who were pessimistic about a peaceful resolution of the dispute were willing to use the typical colonial means of petitioning to redress grievances; if nothing else, it helped preserve congressional unity by not rushing the fainthearted and ambivalent. George left few doubts about his attitude; on August 23, 1775, he proclaimed the colonies in a state of rebellion.

Reluctantly Congress began to accept the likelihood that it would have to accept foreign assistance or possibly even foreign recognition. The establishment of the Secret Committee on September 18 and the Committee of Secret Correspondence on November 29 was a tentative step in that direction. The month after Bonvouloir's visit, Thomas Paine's fiery pamphlet *Common Sense* explained the logic of declaring independence. Congress was held back by the need for unanimity of the states. Some state legislatures like the Pennsylvania Assembly were reluctant to take the final step.

In the interim Congress appointed Connecticut delegate Silas Deane to travel to France to obtain arms. Once arrived, he cooperated with Beaumarchais and passed out commissions in the Continental army to European volunteers. Some of them, like the marquis de Lafayette, would prove valuable, but many did little but compete with American candidates for the few available officer positions. In addition to his lack of common sense, Deane was involved in more than just fulfilling his mission. After graduating from Yale, Deane had been hired to tutor a young man named Edward Bancroft, who eventually found his way to London after establishing a scientific and literary reputation. Deane reencountered Bancroft in Paris and established a partnership to use inside information to play the London stock market. Unknown to Deane, Bancroft also was being paid by the British secret service to deliver information.[5]

By removing roadblocks like the Pennsylvania Assembly, those Americans favoring independence finally managed to obtain favorable instructions for all the state delegations in Congress.[6] On July 4, 1776, Congress approved a Declaration of Independence. It represented a change of attitude not only toward Great Britain but also toward France. By driving France from the North American continent, Britain had cooled (although not completely eliminated) Americans' hatred and suspicion of France, in spite of the long history of colonial rivalry and France's different society, government, and religion.[7] As an accompaniment to the Declaration of Independence, Congress also prepared a draft Treaty of Alliance, mostly the work of John Adams. The draft treaty reflected America's overvaluation of the importance of its trade and its continuing suspicion of France and of military alliances in general.[8] It offered France a share of American trade and the promise of neutrality but not joint action should Britain declare war on France.

The first step to obtaining such a commercial alliance was to elect negotiators. Congress selected three commissioners: Deane, already in France, Arthur Lee, a radical American colonial agent still in England, and Benjamin Franklin, who earlier in the year had risked his life in undertaking a winter mission to Montreal. The three supposedly were equals, but because of Deane's shadiness and Lee's tactlessness, Franklin became the most important member of the delegation. Franklin was able to reassure French aristocrats that they need not fear American revolutionaries. Accustomed to dealing with the elite of England, the witty, charming, patient, and conciliatory Franklin was the perfect face of revolution. Beneath the surface, however, Franklin was among the most zealous and hard line of revolutionaries. He hated George III, who not only had made war on Americans but also had separated Franklin from his beloved son, William, the Loyalist governor of New Jersey.[9] Soon after Franklin sailed from Philadelphia on October 27, 1776, to join his colleagues, the city was placed in peril by the British army. During the latter half of 1776, the British came close to crushing the Continental army and perhaps dooming America's recently declared independence.

TWELVE

The British Might Have Crushed
the Continental Army

The day before Congress gave final approval to the Declaration of Independence, some 9,000 British troops commanded by General William Howe began landing on Staten Island. They were the first wave of the largest expeditionary force Britain had ever sent outside of Europe.

This massive effort was largely the work of the new secretary of state for the American colonies, Lord George Germain, and First Lord of the Admiralty John Montagu, Earl of Sandwich. Both men were reliable hardliners toward the Americans and were extremely industrious; Sandwich's habit of working at his desk through mealtimes led to his requesting salt (corned) beef and bread, which became known as a sandwich. He had alternated between the admiralty and the foreign office for decades, including negotiating the Treaty of Aix-la-Chapelle of 1748. In contrast, Germain had long been relegated to Parliament. At the 1759 Battle of Minden, Germain (then George Sackville before changing his name to receive an inheritance) commanded the British cavalry. He failed to promptly execute a confusing order from Ferdinand of Brunswick and was court-martialed and dismissed from the service. Both he and Sandwich were superb administrators but less capable in formulating and executing strategy.[1]

The greatest initial challenge for the British was finding enough troops. As in 1748 and 1755, they turned to the Russians, but Empress Catherine II refused. Britain was successful, though, at hiring 16,500 troops from Hesse-Kassel and Brunswick, which had provided troops for Ferdinand of Brunswick's army in the Seven Years' War. It also hired 1,600 troops from Hesse-Hanau and Waldeck and used troops from Hanover to garrison Gibraltar and Minorca, freeing British troops for use in America. Some 10,000 troops from Britain, Ireland, and Germany were sent to reinforce Canada in 1776, and 16,500 were sent to Halifax to join the garrison that had been evacuated from Boston in April, preparatory to sailing to New York Harbor. By mid-August the Germans had arrived, and some 25,000 troops were assembled on Staten Island, a portion of the troops having been delayed by an unsuccessful attack on Charleston, South Carolina.[2] The British, in contrast, had economized on the navy, sending enough ships to support the army but not enough to simultaneously blockade the long American coast.[3]

The British attack on New York long had been expected. It was the second largest city in America (behind only Philadelphia) and had a magnificent harbor and access to New England, New Jersey, Pennsylvania, and the Loyalists of the Hudson River valley. It was the opposite of Boston, a great place from which to mount an offensive, but very difficult to defend. Washington had only about 15,000 men to defend the city and its approaches. About half of his men were on Long Island when on August 22 the British landed 15,000 men south of the American lines. The experienced British and German troops soon outflanked the lengthy American defense line and drove the panicked Americans back to a shallow enclave on Brooklyn Heights, inflicting 1,500 or 2,000 casualties against 300 or 400 of their own.

This was a great opportunity for Howe. The first American reaction was to reinforce Brooklyn Heights, where 9,000 soldiers eventually were trapped. Had Howe attacked promptly, he could have captured the entire force and inflicted a poten-

The Continental Army

tially fatal blow to the Continental army. This would have left the British free to conduct a police action against individual communities and their militias. Howe's experience of the frontal attack on Breed's Hill, however, made him so cautious that he decided to besiege the Americans. Luckily Washington's army included two regiments of former sailors, including one from Marblehead, Massachusetts, commanded by the superb John Glover. On the stormy night of August 29-30, they began silently rowing troops across the East River to Manhattan. They were not finished by daybreak, but by good fortune the morning was foggy enough to disguise the remainder of the evacuation. When British patrols arrived, they found the American lines vacant.

Howe soon had another chance to trap part of Washington's army. On September 15 he landed 4,000 men on the east side of Manhattan (near what today is 34th Street), scattering the American defenders. Had the British quickly advanced the three miles to the Hudson, they could have trapped 3,500 American soldiers in New York City to the south. They failed to close the trap, and Washington reunited his army at Harlem Heights.

A month later Howe made another attempt to trap Washington by landing at Pell's Point (now at the northeast tip of the Bronx). Again Glover saved Washington. His regiment's stout resistance slowed the British long enough for Washington to evacuate Harlem Heights. He retreated to White Plains where Howe pushed the American troops back, but bad weather prevented Howe from achieving a decisive victory. When on November 1 he resumed his advance, Washington's army had escaped.[4]

General Guy Carleton, the British commander in Canada, also was unsuccessful. After driving the remnants of the invading American army from Canada, it appeared he would have little trouble in at least recapturing Fort Ticonderoga. Although the American army was too weak to stop him, Carleton still needed to control Lake Champlain. He engaged in a furious shipbuilding race with Benedict Arnold, now commanding the American northern front. Carleton built the stronger fleet and defeated Arnold's ships off Valcour Island on October 11. Arnold had delayed Carleton such a long time, though, that he felt it was too late in the season to besiege Fort Ticonderoga, not realizing it was almost defenseless. Carleton abandoned the dilapidated Fort Crown Point (on the former site of Fort St. Frédéric), which he had occupied, and returned to Canada.[5]

By early November Washington could believe that he too had escaped disaster. He split his army into four parts to prevent any further British advance, but he had made a serious mistake. When he evacuated Manhattan, he left behind a 3,000-man garrison at Fort Washington on the northern tip of the island in order to prevent British ships from sailing up the Hudson. After failing to win a decisive victory at White Plains, Howe doubled back to Manhattan. Fort Washington was weaker than it looked. On November 16 he captured it with its whole garrison and then crossed the Hudson to capture its sister fortification, Fort Lee, which was full of supplies and munitions for the Continental army.

This was a demoralizing defeat for the exhausted Continental army and its commander. Washington's army was in more danger than ever. It retreated across New Jersey, barely outrunning the pursuing British. Only after crossing the Delaware River into Pennsylvania and making sure the British did not have the boats to follow was Washington's army safe.

He faced another danger, however. His army's short-term enlistments were due to expire on December 31, meaning much of his army was liable to melt away. Without firing a shot, the British could achieve their objective of destroying the Continental army, and American independence would depend on what we now call guerrilla warfare. American morale was at so low a point that the loyalty of northern New

Jersey was wavering under British occupation. Washington needed to regain the initiative, restore American morale, and drive the British back to New York.

Fortunately, it was now the British who had made a blunder. They had established a chain of posts along the New Jersey side of the Delaware to protect their gains. Some thirty miles up the Delaware from Philadelphia was a post at Trenton manned by only 1,500 Hessians. Washington planned to cross the Delaware at three points to attack it, using cargo boats to carry troops and ferries to carry cannon. He would personally lead a crossing north of Trenton with 2,400 experienced troops.

In bad weather on the night of December 25–26, 1776, Washington's force successfully crossed the Delaware, but his other two columns were unable to master the icy river. Luckily the Hessians were exhausted from patrolling and were caught by surprise. Washington's force killed or captured most of the garrison, while suffering few casualties except for a future president of the United States, a wounded young Virginia officer named James Monroe. It then returned to Pennsylvania.

The victory was not sufficient to guarantee that Washington's army would reenlist, so the army returned to Trenton a few days later. This time an 8,000-man British detachment from Princeton rushed to attack him. The British force, commanded by General Charles Cornwallis, slightly outnumbered Washington's. When it arrived late in the afternoon of January 2, Cornwallis committed it piecemeal. It was unable to cross a creek south of Trenton, separating it from Washington's army before night fell. By now a master of escape, Washington slipped away and the next day routed the British garrison at Princeton, killing, wounding, or capturing almost half of its 1,200 men. His army then eluded Cornwallis by marching north to safety at Morristown in the hills of northern New Jersey. The British withdrew their scattered New Jersey garrisons to the coast opposite New York

City. Both armies now rested as the campaign finally came to an end.[6]

The battles of Trenton and Princeton were a major turning point in the war. The American accomplishments of the previous half-year were hairbreadth escapes largely due to Howe's caution. Trenton and Princeton were an even greater affirmation of American military prowess than Bunker Hill had been, because they were won by attacking rather than defending a position. Washington had finally shown he could advance as well as retreat. His army at Morristown was far smaller than the British army at New York, but it could be rebuilt because Washington had shown that the British were not invincible. Washington became a prodigy in the eyes of French military leaders and aristocrats, which would be of assistance to Franklin and Vergennes. The British campaign was not a total failure. They still held New York and in December captured Newport, Rhode Island, but they had lost northern New Jersey and Lake Champlain and would face longer odds in 1777. Meanwhile the great dockyards of Brest, Rochefort, and Toulon were bringing closer the day France would be able to intervene.

THIRTEEN

Louis XVI Could Have Pulled Back from War

On December 3, 1776, Benjamin Franklin left the Continental navy warship *Reprisal* and was rowed ashore at the small Breton port of Auray.[1] Accompanying him were his sixteen-year-old grandson, William Temple Franklin, the illegitimate son of Loyalist governor William Franklin, and his seven-year-old grandson, Benjamin Franklin Bache, the son of his daughter, Sally. The former was to serve as Franklin's secretary, while the latter was being sent to receive a European education and would eventually be sent to a boarding school in Protestant Geneva. The three traveled to Paris where they found Deane and soon were joined by Lee. The American commissioners then met with the Spanish ambassador, representatives of the Farmers General (the bankers who held a monopoly on tobacco sales in France and soon signed a contract to purchase American tobacco), Vergennes's undersecretary Conrad-Alexandre Gérard, and, in secret, Vergennes himself.

They did not obtain the huge loan or the ships of the line they requested, but Vergennes was willing to help as best as he could while keeping French assistance secret; the naval reconstruction program was not half finished yet, and France dared not risk a premature war with Britain. He arranged luxurious living accommodations for them with a navy contractor in the prosperous village of Passy, halfway between

Paris and Versailles. (The village is now the equally wealthy 16th arrondisement of Paris.) Lee chose to remain in Paris. Vergennes also arranged a banker for them, a brother of the banker who had financed King Gustavus III's coup in Sweden. Best of all, he gave permission for American ships to use French ports and gave the commissioners the first installment of a 2 million livre grant.

Although Franklin had to be kept at arm's length by Vergennes, he had numerous entries into the higher reaches of French society because of his scientific accomplishments, his high rank in the Freemasons, and his neighbors in Passy. He attended meetings of the Académie royale des sciences, the prestigious Neuf Soeurs Masonic lodge (which he eventually headed), and, somewhat later, the Société royale de médecine. Aware of the need to show respect for Vergennes, he avoided contact with Choiseul and, at least publicly, the politically suspect writer Denis Diderot, although he did reestablish contact with his old friend Turgot and met with Voltaire. He kept his distance, too, from the commoners of Paris, despite their fascination with the famous American who dressed like a simple Quaker.[2]

Franklin was kept busy courting the wealthy and influential, but the commissioners' negotiations through Gérard with the French government were so limited and frustrating that Lee, disregarding Franklin's advice, undertook humiliating missions to request help from Spain and Prussia. The French government dared not confide in the commissioners because they knew the unofficial American embassy in Passy was full of British spies; instead, it ignored without explanation the commissioners' rather hectoring memoirs. Franklin was partly responsible for the faulty communication. Although he hated the British, he also had no love for taking security precautions. This breakdown was very dangerous because the commissioners did not understand the French need for caution until their navy was ready. American privateer captains

Louis Could Have Pulled Back

like the celebrated Gustavus Conyngham came to French ports to sell their prizes and recruit crewmen. An irresponsible young messenger named William Carmichael, sent to deliver orders to Conyngham to return to America, instead (possibly under the advice of Deane) suggested he continue cruising for prizes. The British government was so outraged at the privateers that in August 1777 it threatened war unless France expelled all American armed ships, including a squadron of three American warships at St. Malo and Morlaix. The French government was so concerned that it expelled the squadron, recalled its fishing fleet from Newfoundland, and finally sent reinforcements to the French West Indies. One of the American warships was captured and another, the *Reprisal*, which had remained in Europe after delivering Franklin, was lost in a storm while returning to America.[3]

The French government's relations with the commissioners soon resumed their polite but distant pattern. Deane was so frustrated that when Vergennes promised more money but insisted it be kept secret, he suggested on November 27 that the commissioners threaten the French government that the United States would reconcile with Britain unless France agreed to an alliance. Franklin and Lee rejected his idea.[4] Their patience soon would be rewarded because of a combination of news from America and, even more important, the impending completion of France's naval rearmament.

Germain and his colleagues in the British cabinet had hoped to crush the American rebels before France could intervene in the war. Their plans called for new offensives during 1777 in northern New York and in the American middle colonies (or, as the Americans now called them, states). Carleton was retained as governor at Quebec, but he was replaced by Burgoyne as commander of the army sent to capture Albany, a division of authority that created friction. Howe was expected to capture Philadelphia and destroy Washington's army, after which presumably he would send a detachment to join Burgoyne at Albany, sealing off New England from the rest of the colonies. He was not explicitly ordered to do so, however. In any case he left troops at New York to support Burgoyne if needed. This strategy proved too optimistic and overly complicated, largely because of Howe and Burgoyne's failure to cooperate.

Howe decided to go to Philadelphia by sea, although the cabinet did not learn of this until it was too late to question his decision. In June he tried unsuccessfully to lure Washington into battle in New Jersey. The following month he embarked 14,000 troops at New York. Before sailing on July 23, he learned that Burgoyne had captured Fort Ticonderoga; both he and Burgoyne believed the campaign in northern New York was all but won. By the end of the month, his flotilla of warships and transports was in Delaware Bay. He then lost his nerve after being warned that sailing to the head of the bay would risk shipwreck or a contested troop landing. Instead he sailed south to the entrance of Chesapeake Bay. He was not able to disembark his troops until August 25 at the head of that bay, more than fifty miles from Philadelphia. During the voyage twenty-seven soldiers had died and more than 300 horses had either died or had to be killed.

During Howe's march to Philadelphia, he encountered Washington's army of 16,000 men at Brandywine Creek and outflanked it, inflicting more than 1,000 casualties, twice his own. The Americans fought bravely, though, and Howe, like a typical European general, henceforth preferred to maneuver Washington out of position rather than fighting him again. He did so and was able to march unopposed into Philadelphia on September 26. The Continental Congress escaped.

Washington wanted another chance to defeat the British and on October 4 attacked Howe's advanced post at Germantown, north of Philadelphia. His attack plans were too complicated and failed, with both sides suffering losses similar to those at Brandywine.

Howe was not yet safe. He could only provision his army by bringing supplies up the Delaware. The Americans had forts along the river and gunboats in it, which the British had to clear away. In doing so the British lost a ship of the line, the only one destroyed by Americans during the war. Howe's army now could enjoy the comforts of Philadelphia, while west of the city the Americans suffered through the winter at their makeshift camp at Valley Forge.[5]

Although Howe had captured Philadelphia, he was unable to send reinforcements to Burgoyne. In contrast, Washington sent reinforcements to fight Burgoyne, including one of his best units, 600 crack riflemen commanded by Colonel Daniel Morgan.

Burgoyne's campaign started well enough. The Americans did not contest the passage of his 8,000-man army up Lake Champlain to Fort Ticonderoga, preferring to build ships on Lake George. The fort's garrison of 2,200 men was too small to defend all the hills overlooking it. Burgoyne was able easily to force its evacuation on the night of July 4–5. He pursued the retreating Americans as far as Skenesborough, thirty miles south of Fort Ticonderoga. Here Burgoyne made a serious mistake. Disregarding the lessons to be drawn from Braddock's and Forbes's difficult marches during the previous war, he decided to construct a road south to Fort Edward on the Hudson rather than backtrack to Lake Champlain and Lake George. Proceeding at a mile a day, it took him three vital weeks. He then spent ten days assembling supplies and loading them on small boats for passage down the Hudson. Downriver he crossed to the west bank while detaching 1,000 men to seize a rebel supply base at Bennington, twenty miles east of the river. Rebel militiamen, outraged at Burgoyne's bombastic threats and use of Native Americans, surrounded and destroyed the detachment. Another British force of 2,000 soldiers, Loyalists, and Native Americans sent east via the Mohawk River to aid Burgoyne had to turn back.

Once west of the Hudson, Burgoyne's severely depleted army had to reach Albany or perish. General Clinton at New York sent troops and boats up the Hudson, capturing the American forts at the Hudson Highlands, but they too had to turn back. American cannon on the riverbanks prevented them from getting closer than forty-five miles south of Albany. North of Albany the new American commander, the popular Horatio Gates, constructed a strong defense line west of the river. Burgoyne, badly outnumbered, was unable to break through the defenses. Near the village of Saratoga he surrendered his 6,000 survivors on October 17 to Gates, who had once served with him in the same regiment of the British army.[6]

Although Saratoga was a major triumph, it does not seem in retrospect to have been quite as important as Bunker Hill, Trenton, or Yorktown. As long as Washington's army remained intact, it seems unlikely that the British could have found the necessary troops to cut off New England from the other states, even had Burgoyne reached Albany and established communications with Clinton at New York City. American militia had demonstrated at Bennington their ability to destroy British detachments like the ones that would have been needed along the 300 miles from Montreal to New York. Before the British could control more territory, they needed to destroy Washington's army. Thus Burgoyne's strategy was inherently flawed.

The Battle of Saratoga is renowned above all for its supposed diplomatic consequences. The news of the victory that reached Vergennes and the commissioners on December 4, 1777, did contribute to the conclusion of the French alliance two months later.[7] It was probably not as important a factor, however, as the impending completion of the naval rebuilding program. In early 1777 the French ambassador at the Spanish court reported that Spain would have fifty-two ships of the line ready to serve by the year's end and another

Louis Could Have Pulled Back

seven that would be ready by the end of 1778. French negotiations to procure their help were second in importance only to the negotiations with the United States. At the beginning of May 1777, the ambassador told the Spaniards that by the end of the year France would have enough supplies on hand to make war. On July 23, Louis's council of state approved a report prepared by Joseph-Mathias Gérard arguing that for the present France should assist the Americans financially, but eventually it should make a secret treaty recognizing their independence and promising to intervene openly if needed. The French ports should prepare as if war with Britain would commence in March 1778. On the same day Louis approved sending a memoir to Spain saying there was no obstacle to their going to war with Britain as soon as the French fishing fleet returned, but that they should not wait past January or February 1778, lest the opportunity be lost. In a separate letter of July 26, Vergennes instructed his ambassador to warn the Spaniards that American negotiations with Britain were likely at the end of the 1777 campaign in America. Spain, in reply, urged caution, and the dissipation of the privateering crisis in August caused the discussions with Spain to taper off. Nevertheless the correspondence with Spain indicates that the news of Saratoga arrived at just the time France had indicated a decision should be made about abandoning limited intervention in favor of preparing to enter the war.[8]

The timing of the transition reflects the impending completion of the program of ship overhauls and dockyard replenishment. All but one of the seven ships of the line still in overhaul at the end of 1777 were in service when war began at the beginning of the summer of 1778; new ships began overhauls, but when war began, only three ships of the line were not in service because they were undergoing overhauls.[9] There were three remaining obstacles to making an American alliance: the need for America to agree to assist France in case of a Franco-British war, the need to make an attempt to gain Spanish participation in the war, and the need to overcome Louis XVI's remaining scruples about going to war and hence postponing domestic reforms.[10]

Once discussions began, the American commissioners took only five days to assure France that if France offered a treaty of commerce, the United States would not agree to any peace with Britain that did not recognize American independence. They also promised Gérard that Louis would find the Americans "faithful and firm Allies" (a concession that Congress had long since recognized might be necessary).[11] Conversely Vergennes realized that Spain would not immediately join the alliance when he learned on December 31 that their vital treasure fleet from Vera Cruz, Mexico, had not yet arrived. A secret article in the subsequent Franco-American Treaty of Alliance gave Charles III the right to join "at such time as he shall judge proper." The real obstacle was King Louis XVI. To overcome his reluctance, Vergennes, with the tacit assistance of Franklin, engaged in another round of melodramatic worry (which at some level might have been at least a little bit genuine). Vergennes had worked his way with the king often enough that success was likely, but there was still a chance the king might balk, in which case American independence would eventually have been at terrible risk.

Vergennes used his usual gambit of warning of the dangers if France *didn't* act. He warned that if France didn't become more involved, the British and Americans might jointly attack the French West Indies. Vergennes's warnings were far-fetched. There was no reason for the United States to join in an attack on the French West Indies; the United States had no desire for its own West Indian colonies, and once reassured that France had no desire for territory in North America, it had no reason to attack France.

A somewhat more genuine danger was posed when North sent a peace commission to offer Congress independence provided America still complied with the Navigation

Louis Could Have Pulled Back

Acts. Still there was little real chance that Congress would accept anything short of full independence on the morrow of a great military victory. (The peace commissioners' terms were unanimously rejected by Congress, although it had already learned of the Franco-American alliance.) On his own, Franklin reinforced Vergennes's warnings about an American reconciliation with Britain. North, panicked by the news of Saratoga, sent an emissary, former New Hampshire governor Paul Wentworth, to sound out Franklin about making peace. Franklin gave him no satisfaction, but made sure their meeting became public knowledge. (Two amateur peacemakers showed up as well.) This piece of theater was probably directed at Vergennes, but it undoubtedly reached the proper audience, Louis XVI.

At virtually the last moment, a new problem arose. A disputed inheritance gave Austria a chance of obtaining most of Bavaria, threatening the European balance of power or an Austro-Prussian war that might involve France. France was too close to a war with Britain to get involved in a European war, even if Vergennes had been interested, which he was not. France chose to remain neutral, while using the Austro-French alliance to restrain Austria. Austria and Prussia mobilized their armies for a bloodless confrontation known as the Potato War (after the rival armies' chief victims). In 1779 Russia intervened on Prussia's behalf, and the Austrians backed down.[12]

On January 7, 1778, Vergennes finally won the king's approval for formal negotiations. There were actually two treaties involved, a commercial treaty called the Treaty of Amity and Commerce, as well as a Treaty of Alliance. There were no difficulties with the former because the French gave the commissioners everything they wanted, asking only permission to trade with the United States. (They incorrectly assumed that they could compete with the British on even terms for American markets.) The latter treaty made the commissioners nervous because the French wished it to be one of defensive alliance, the commissioners fearing the French might back out. Actually the French wished only to be able to choose for military reasons when to open hostilities, assuming it would be easy at the time to provoke the British into opening hostilities first (and hence preventing their obtaining Dutch help under the British-Dutch defensive alliance).

The formal negotiations with the commissioners took less than a month. On February 6 both treaties were signed.[13] American independence would henceforth depend not only on what happened on American battlefields but also on what happened when the rebuilt French navy finally saw action.

Louis Could Have Pulled Back

FOURTEEN

Spain Might Not Have Joined the War

On March 13, 1778, barely a month after the French treaties with the United States were signed, the French ambassador to the British court announced the signing of the Treaty of Amity and Commerce (although not the signing of the Treaty of Alliance). The British government could no longer ignore France's involvement and immediately broke diplomatic relations. France reciprocated, announcing to the world its recognition of the United States, a step that reassured the commissioners and doomed the British peace commission to America. It reinforced the message on March 20, when the king formally received the commissioners at court, followed soon thereafter by their presentation to the queen.

France was now free to prepare openly for war. The dockyards were ordered to prepare ships for service, including the navy's largest ships, the *Bretagne*, the *Ville-de-Paris*, and the *Duc-de-Bourgogne*. On March 7 the king approved a convoy to bring back merchant shipping (with its many trained sailors) from the West Indies, giving France a head start over Britain in manning its navy; many of the sailors Britain needed were in the West Indies and East Indies and would not be available for this year's campaign. (It also helped that France, unlike Britain, maintained a registry of sailors, some of whom could be called up for immediate service.)[1]

France also could begin to implement its war strategy, making use of its temporary near parity in ships of the line and its great ports on both the Atlantic coast and in the Mediterranean. The ships at Brest and Rochefort could be sent across the Atlantic to attack the British West Indies or New York, or could be used to intercept incoming British convoys, or could even cover an invasion of England. As the British did not have a fleet in the Mediterranean, ships from Toulon could be sent across the Atlantic or join an invasion of England. British uncertainty over French strategy gave France the advantage of surprise and a head start in conducting whatever plan it chose.

The strategy it picked was extraordinarily similar to the one that it had picked in 1756, when the Toulon fleet was used to surprise Minorca. Even the size of the Toulon fleet was almost identical. This time its objective was not Minorca, which was reserved for future capture by Spain, but New York. The British garrison at this vital port and the supplies assembled there were protected by only six regular ships of the line and four 50-gun ships. If they were captured or driven away, New York could be blockaded until hunger forced its surrender. Admiral Charles-Henri, comte d'Estaing, sailed for New York from Toulon on the evening of April 13, 1778, with eleven ships of the line, a 50-gun ship, and five frigates. Aboard his flagship were Conrad-Alexandre Gérard, who had been chosen as the first French minister plenipotentiary to the United States, and Silas Deane, who had been recalled by Congress to explain his prolific granting of Continental army commissions; John Adams was being sent to France as Deane's replacement. Meanwhile, to confuse the British, the navy prepared a fleet of thirty ships of the line and two 50-gun ships at Brest.[2]

The British cabinet was unsure of how to respond. If it sent a squadron to New York and the Toulon squadron came to Brest, the French might have enough ships to cover an inva-

Spain Joins the War

sion of England; as in 1756 the French used encampments along the Atlantic coast to emphasize the threat. Conversely, if Britain kept its ships in home waters, the Toulon squadron could overwhelm the ships at New York. Germain discounted the danger of invasion and wished to protect New York, while Sandwich, influenced by Admiral Augustus Keppel, the timid commander of the Channel Fleet, feared invasion and persuaded the cabinet to delay sending reinforcements to New York until it was certain the Toulon squadron was not sailing to Brest. Thus a squadron of thirteen ships of the line for New York commanded by Admiral John Byron waited until a frigate arrived to report that the French squadron had passed the Straits of Gibraltar, sailing west.[3]

The British were fortunate to escape disaster. D'Estaing had a several weeks head start, and "Foul Weather Jack" Byron's squadron was scattered by a storm. The commander of the squadron at New York was Richard Howe, who had negotiated with Franklin in 1774-75. Howe, a superb tactician, saved his squadron by stationing it off Sandy Hook, New Jersey, protected by shore batteries. D'Estaing, fearing the water was too shallow for his largest ships, gave up the attempt and sailed to attack the 6,700-man British garrison at Newport. An American army of 10,000 militia and soldiers was assembled to assist, but before they could attack, Howe arrived to save the garrison, having been joined by one of Byron's ships of the line and another from the West Indies. As d'Estaing and Howe maneuvered for position, a storm struck their squadrons. D'Estaing sailed to Boston for repairs. While he was there, Byron, who had finally relieved Howe at New York, came to attack him but was hit by another storm. On November 4 d'Estaing sailed for Martinique.[4]

Meanwhile the British adjusted their own war strategy in order to counter the supposed French threat to the British West Indies. The cabinet decided to attack the island of St. Lucia, just south of the main French base at Martinique. To provide the necessary 5,000 troops, the British evacuated Philadelphia and marched to New York, fighting a heavy skirmish with Washington's army at Monmouth while en route. On the same day that d'Estaing sailed from Boston, the troops for attacking St. Lucia sailed from New York under a weak naval escort. Narrowly escaping d'Estaing, they captured the island.[5]

The only naval battle during 1778 occurred not in American waters but off the French coast soon after three French frigates engaged in battle the entire British Channel Fleet, giving France the opportunity to claim that Britain had started the war. Here it was the French navy that was in danger. It had a long history of losing major battles, and although the French fleet at Brest had the same number of ships as the British Home Fleet (often called the Western Squadron), they carried fewer cannon. When the Brest fleet sailed for the western approaches to the British Isles on July 8, 1778, it left behind no ships as a reserve. The closest French ships of the line were four that d'Estaing had left behind at Toulon. Although the French commander was ordered not to seek battle, it was almost inevitable. This was Sartine's finest hour. Even though most naval battles were inconclusive, it still took enormous courage to risk all the ships of France's Atlantic Fleet, much like the Royal Air Force putting all of its available planes in the air during the height of the Battle of Britain. When the battle took place off the French island of Ushant (near Brest), the two fleets sailed past each other in opposite directions with indecisive results. The French suffered more casualties and the British more damage to their ships, but no ships were lost by either side. The battle nevertheless was of enormous psychological importance. The French gained confidence while the British fleet was thrown in turmoil when Admiral Keppel and his subordinate, Admiral Huge Palliser, blamed each other for the battle's unsatisfactory outcome.[6]

Spain Joins the War

In spite of the navy's excellent performance at the Battle of Ushant, the campaign of 1778 was a French failure. They had wasted their chance of winning a decisive victory before the British could fully man their navy. On July 1, 1779, the British would have ninety ships of the line (including 50-gun ships) in service, two dozen more than a year earlier, thanks chiefly to the increase in the number of available crewmen. France would have sixty-three, an increase of less than a dozen. Without the help of the Spanish navy, France stood little chance of ever reducing the odds. (Spain had fifty-eight ships of the line in use on July 1, 1779.)[7]

Spain's help would not come cheaply. Charles III had no love for rebels against a monarchy, as he had his own empire in the Western Hemisphere. His motive for giving financial aid to the Americans had been to keep their revolt alive and to drain British strength, the motive that Vergennes falsely claimed was also his own. (Fortunately, the Spanish governor of Louisiana, the great soldier Bernardo de Gálvez, was more sympathetic to the Americans.)[8] What Charles most cared about was obtaining the return of Gibraltar and Minorca to Spain. To obtain them he offered Britain Spain's neutrality in the war. The offer was tempting, but no British leader was willing to brave English public opinion. During 1778 France had tried unsuccessfully to convince Charles III of the advantages of American independence to Spain and had been solicitous of Spanish feelings, even asking Spain's approval for sending d'Estaing to New York. Now that the campaign of 1778 had failed, France had to pay whatever price Spain demanded. On December 5 Vergennes warned Louis that Spain's pretensions were gigantic but that France had to take some risks to gain an alliance and it was too late to argue over details.[9]

The subsequent negotiations took four months before a convention concerning joint war aims was signed at Charles's palace at Aranjuez on April 12, 1779.[10] It would come into effect only if Britain rejected Spain's final mediation offer (that is, Spain's demands).

The war aims basically were dictated by Spain. France had to promise not to make peace until Spain obtained Gibraltar. The Spanish chief minister, José Moñino y Redondo, conde de Floridablanca, tried unsuccessfully to add Minorca and East Florida to the requirement. France obtained in return a Spanish agreement not to make peace until France gained the right to fortify the privateering port of Dunkirk, denied since 1713. Spain, however, did acknowledge France's obligation not to make peace until the British recognized American independence. Spain agreed not to make peace until this obligation was fulfilled, although Spain would not recognize American independence until Britain did so.

Equally important to Spain was France's agreement in the convention to furnish all the troops and part of the naval escort for an invasion of England. Charles III remembered the damage Britain had done to the Spanish empire in 1762 by capturing Havana and Manila. He feared that a lengthy war would endanger Spain's extensive colonies. He was as anxious to end the war in a single campaign as France had been in 1778.

The Convention of Aranjuez was critical to the survival of American independence. Without it the French navy inevitably would have been overwhelmed. Without the French navy, the United States eventually would have been cut off from foreign markets, money, and military supplies and blockaded into surrender or a destructive compromise peace. The Continental army, short on food and pay, had been hard pressed to survive its encampment at Valley Forge; it could not have endured such shortages indefinitely. Instead Spain provided invaluable assistance to the allied war effort. It did not do so, however, without surviving great danger itself.

FIFTEEN

Spain Might Have Made Peace with Britain

L ouis XVI agreed to Spain's demands to invade England, but limited the invasion's size and scope.[1] Some 20,000 soldiers, assembled in St. Malo and Le Havre, were to be carried to England by 115 to 150 transports. (The number of soldiers later was slightly enlarged.) Vergennes feared that attacking London would frighten the neutral powers of Europe, so France chose the Isle of Wight off the south coast of England as its objective. From there the invaders could organize the bombardment of the great British naval port of Portsmouth. It was hoped this would cause a financial panic and force the British government to make peace. Vergennes did not want to depose George III. He wished only to chastise Britain for its support of Russia by depriving it of a portion of its power, the partial monopoly of American trade. It might then even cooperate with France in protecting the weaker states of eastern Europe.

The most imposing part of the plan was the naval escort. A huge force was needed to gain control of the waters off the English coast so that the transports could arrive safely. The allies used the greatest fleet ever collected during the age of sail, thirty-six Spanish ships of the line and thirty French ships of the line. Spanish warships were among the world's best, particularly those built in Havana of tropical hardwoods, including the 114-gun *Santísima Trinidad*, the world's most powerful warship.[2] On the other hand, Spanish crews largely were untrained and its captains inexperienced in fleet maneuvers. Moreover the difficulties in combining so many ships from various ports and then sailing together in unfamiliar seas proved too much to overcome. The Spanish contingent from Cadiz had to struggle against contrary winds and did not reach the rendezvous point until July 22–23, 1779. At the beginning of August the combined fleet sailed for the English coast. When it reached the area off Plymouth in mid-month, it created a near panic, since it had slipped by the British Home Fleet to the west. By now the target of the invasion had been shifted to remote Cornwall on the southwestern tip of England. The transports could not sail, however, until the threat of the thirty-nine ships of the line in the British fleet was neutralized. Unable to catch the British, short on supplies, and swept by disease, the allied fleet finally gave up and sailed to Brest in early September. Although the attempt failed, it had a lasting impact on the war. In 1780 and 1781 a combined Franco-Spanish fleet cruised to the south of England, forcing the British to keep many ships at home for fear of another invasion attempt (although none was planned). This helped give the French and Spanish navies opportunities in the Western Hemisphere.

There was an immediate offshoot of the invasion attempt. During his wars with England Louis XIV had used his own funds to outfit privateering squadrons as a business venture. Louis XVI outfitted such a squadron in 1779, using privateers, a Continental navy frigate, and French warships, partly as a diversion to help the main fleet and partly to give an opportunity to the famed Continental navy captain John Paul Jones. The naval contractor Jacques-Donatien Leray de Chaumont (Franklin's landlord) even provided Jones with a converted East Indies ship that was renamed the *Bonhomme Richard*, after Franklin's pen name, "Poor Richard." On September 20 Jones's squadron encountered a large British convoy off

Spain Might Have Made Peace

the east coast of England. The convoy escaped, but the *Bon-homme Richard* captured a large escorting frigate, the *Serapis*, before sinking. The squadron escaped to a Dutch naval base before eventually returning to France. The *Serapis* was bought at auction by Louis XVI, but later was shipwrecked in the Indian Ocean.[3]

Spain did not abandon the war after the failed invasion. Vergennes rebuffed its attempt to commit France to another attempt by demanding Spain share its cost and provide more ships. Instead, Spain announced that it would reinforce its squadron blockading Gibraltar. Fifteen of its ships of the line left Brest on November 9. They did not arrive in time. Admiral George Rodney brought a squadron of twenty-one ships of the line to provision Gibraltar, catching by surprise eleven Spanish ships of the line blockading the fortress. He captured four of them and destroyed two others. He then sailed to reinforce the West Indies with four ships of the line and sent the rest back to England. Eventually the Spanish blockade of Gibraltar would greatly help France by repeatedly tying down a major portion of the British Home Fleet in escorting replenishment convoys. This first replenishment, however, inflicted so demoralizing a defeat on the Spanish navy that for a month Charles III could not decide what to do.[4]

Things were not going well for the United States or France, either. Clinton, who had replaced Howe as the British commander in America, was inactive in the summer of 1779 except for an incursion into the Hudson Highlands and a raid on Virginia. Washington was able to detach 4,000 of his 12,000 troops to conduct a scorched earth campaign against the Iroquois. Meanwhile a small force of Virginians under George Rogers Clark was fighting a brutal war in the Illinois Country against the British and Native Americans. A serious British threat to the American south developed during 1779, though. At the beginning of the year, a small British force from East Florida captured Savannah and then threatened

Charleston. D'Estaing remained in the West Indies until the start of the hurricane season, having failed to recapture St. Lucia (although he did capture the rich sugar-producing island of Grenada). In September he brought his squadron and 3,500 troops, including 600 free black volunteers, to America. In conjunction with a similar number of Americans, they besieged and then assaulted Savannah. During the October 9 assault, d'Estaing was wounded. After it failed, the French squadron departed and the Americans retreated.[5]

The stalemate in both the north and south seems to have overcome Washington's hesitations about having French troops on American soil. He wrote Lafayette, who was on leave in France, that he would welcome a French expeditionary force, preferably commanded by the young Frenchman. Lafayette informed Maurepas of the letter on January 12, 1780, or soon thereafter. By the end of the month, plans were readied to send six ships of the line and 3,000 or 4,000 troops to North America. The council of state gave its approval on February 2, but named Rochambeau to command the troops.[6]

By coincidence a huge convoy of seventeen ships of the line and 4,500 troops left Brest for Martinique at the beginning of February, with 2,000 of the troops being promised to Spain for its use. Rodney was still at Gibraltar, so their departure was unopposed, the first of several sailings made easy because the Home Fleet was being used to help succor Gibraltar. Finally at the end of February, Charles III informed France of his intention to send twelve to fourteen ships of the line and 8,000 to 10,000 troops to the Western Hemisphere.

The French convoys to the Caribbean and North America and the Spanish convoy to the Caribbean were vital to the allies taking the offensive against Britain in the Western Hemisphere. Had Britain intercepted any of them, the outcome of the war easily could have been different; it was one of Britain's greatest opportunities.

The first French convoy reached Martinique on March 22,

Spain Might Have Made Peace

1780, a few days before Rodney's arrival at Barbados. Admiral Luc-Urbain de Bouexic, comte de Guichen's French squadron subsequently made unsuccessful attempts to attack Barbados and St. Lucia, as well as fighting three naval battles against Rodney before taking a huge convoy back to Europe before the onset of the hurricane season.

The most crucial convoy was the Spanish one. Its loss probably would have knocked Spain out of the war, which would have been followed almost inevitably by the defeat of France and the collapse of the American rebellion. It sailed from Cadiz on April 28 with 146 merchant ships and transports carrying 11,000 troops. Its escort of 12 ships of the line was too weak to defend them if it encountered Rodney's fleet of twice its size. The Spaniards decided to stop at the French West Indies to obtain provisions

Rodney knew the Spaniards were coming and was waiting off Martinique for them. A British frigate spotted the convoy on June 5, but it turned north toward Guadeloupe, off which it found the French fleet. Later it proceeded to the French colony of St. Domingue (now Haiti) and then Cuba. Wars are not won just by battles. The Spanish convoy's change of course may have saved American independence.

The French had difficulty finding transports for Rochambeau's little army, but rather than wait, it sailed from Brest on May 2 with 5,500 troops and seven ships of the line. (Another 2,500 men were to follow, but were prevented from doing so by the danger of British interception.) The British knew that the convoy was bound for North America, but not its exact destination. They sent a squadron of six ships of the line to intercept it. It arrived to join four ships of the line in New York just as the French convoy reached America. The previous autumn d'Estaing's voyage to America had frightened Clinton into evacuating Newport, which is where the French convoy arrived on July 12. By the time the British were ready to attack, the French had fortified Newport. Rodney soon visited New York, but he left more than a dozen ships of the line in the Caribbean, where they suffered terrible damage during a huge October hurricane.[7]

To complete the naval successes of 1780, the combined Franco-Spanish fleet off the south of England captured sixty-one merchant ships worth £1.5 million (35 million livres) off the Azores from a convoy of sixty-seven ships for Jamaica and St. Kitts, the richest prize of the war.[8]

The French and Spanish navies had averted a catastrophe that could have undermined the American Revolution. On land, however, 1780 was a year of British triumph and near American disaster.

Spain Might Have Made Peace

SIXTEEN

The British Might Have Captured West Point

The repulse of d'Estaing's attack on Savannah finally gave the British an opportunity to break the stalemate of 1779. In December Clinton decided to attack Charleston. At the end of the month, a fleet of ninety transports sailed from New York. After picking up reinforcements at Savannah and weathering a storm, it arrived at Charleston and began landing troops.[1] On April 1, 1780, Clinton, who accompanied the troops, began constructing siege works. The Continental navy sent to Charleston three of its dwindling number of frigates, and the Continental army sent reinforcements as well, but it was in vain. The British were experts at siege warfare, and both American soldiers and civilians suffered terribly. On May 10 the 5,700 soldiers and 1,000 sailors defending the city surrendered. Clinton had won revenge for Saratoga.[2]

Once the city was taken, Clinton left his subordinate, Cornwallis, to complete the capture of South Carolina, hoping to then turn it over to Loyalists. Congress named General Horatio Gates to command the Southern Department, but he had only 1,400 Continental soldiers and about 2,500 militiamen. Cornwallis advanced to meet him at Camden, 100 miles north of Charleston. The British gained further revenge for Saratoga, crushing Gates's army on August 16, 1780. Gates fled after the battle, adding further humiliation.

Loyalist units captured American posts in the backcountry, and it now appeared that the British could begin rolling up the American revolt from south to north.[3]

With the Continental army largely reduced to Washington's own men, Clinton prepared what might be a fatal blow. During the previous year Clinton had been humiliated by the American recapture of the post of Stony Point in the Hudson Highlands, thirty miles north of New York City, which he had taken recently. Afterward Washington destroyed the post. Clinton now had a bigger target in mind, the key American fortress of West Point, a dozen miles north of Stony Point. West Point guarded the main supply routes across the Hudson connecting New England with New York and New Jersey. If he could capture it, Washington would have to divide his army in order to watch New York from the west while shielding the newly arrived French troops at Newport to the east. The fortress, located on a cliff above the Hudson, was almost invulnerable, but Clinton hoped to capture it in late 1780 without a fight with the help of its commander, General Benedict Arnold.

Arnold, the most audacious of American generals, felt he had not been given enough credit for his contribution to the American victory at Saratoga. While commanding recaptured Philadelphia, he had married the daughter of a prominent Loyalist sympathizer. Now he arranged to help Clinton surprise West Point. His plan might have been successful had not an American patrol captured Clinton's aide, Major John André, his liaison with Arnold. The plan was foiled, and André was executed as a spy. Arnold escaped and joined the British. Clinton's plan to seize West Point overlapped with the repeated failure of the British to mount an amphibious attack on the French at Newport. Because his West Point plot was approaching a climax, he failed to agree to a proposal by Rodney for a joint attack on Newport.

Militarily the loss of West Point would have been a serious blow but not a fatal one. As we shall see, however, the Continental army was at a low point at the end of 1780, and the psychological consequences could have been disastrous.[4]

At least the situation in the south began to improve. The British committed the ultimate atrocity in southern eyes by encouraging slaves to escape and then employing them. Carolinians now eagerly joined bands of irregulars to fight the British and Loyalists. On October 7, 1780, some 1,800 Americans killed or captured a force of 1,000 Loyalists at King's Mountain, just across the border in North Carolina. The war in South Carolina turned increasingly bitter as Patriots and Loyalists burned property and killed each other.[5]

At the beginning of 1781, a new crisis even worse than the possible loss of West Point threatened American independence. Congress was in danger of financial collapse, and the Continental army suddenly appeared ready to disintegrate. Meanwhile the French government, which increasingly was underpinning the American government and economy, faced its own financial peril. There was a serious possibility that 1781 would be the final campaign for both France and the United States.

SEVENTEEN

A Financial Collapse Could Have
Doomed the Revolution

T
he dual financial crisis that threatened the continuation of French aid and the survival of the United
States was long in coming. Indeed it was grounded
in the very natures of the two countries.

The Continental Congress lacked the ability to raise its
own taxes. Instead it was dependent on the states and on foreign loans for its support, and these sources were inadequate.
Congress therefore resorted to printing money to pay for the
war. The American commissioners in 1777 rashly promised
to pay the interest on loan office certificates (equivalent to
war bonds, of which $60 million worth were sold) from the
money they received from France.[1] These held their value,
but the strength of American currency depended on public
confidence that it would not depreciate. This was not sus-
tainable.[2] Congress issued $6 million in paper money during
1775, expecting the states eventually to redeem it by taxation. The amount printed rose continually. By early 1780 it
had emitted $240 million. Another $100 million in military
supply certificates were also issued by late 1781. Naturally
the value of the currency declined in relationship to specie
(coin). (A dollar in specie was worth about five livres or a fifth
of a British pound sterling.) In January 1777, thanks to public enthusiasm for the war, it took only $1.25 in currency to
purchase $1 in specie. By October 1778 it took $5 and then

in 1779 depreciation accelerated: it took $30 in October 1779 and $60 by the following spring. In March 1780 Congress devalued the currency by forty to one, ruining foreign enthusiasts for America like Franklin's landlord, Jacques-Donatien Leray de Chaumont. Franklin, who by now was American minister plenipotentiary in France, responded sympathetically to Vergennes's complaints, but John Adams, who was in France vainly awaiting a call from Britain to negotiate peace, was so confrontational that he had to leave France.[3]

In June 1780 Congress picked the rich financier Robert Morris as superintendent of finance. Morris temporarily alleviated the problem, in part by using his own credit, but Congress increasingly depended on France for the money to keep it going. France extended 3 million livres in loans in 1778, 1 million in 1779, and 4 million in 1780.[4]

Although this was a strain on the king's budget, it was only a small portion of France's war expenses. Normal peacetime expenses for the navy and colonies were about 28 million livres per year. Naval and colonial expenditures were more than 47 million livres in 1776 due to the rearmament program. This increased by 11 million in 1777. Once war started, expenses arose rapidly: 125 million livres in naval and colonial expenses alone during 1778, more than 150 million in 1779, and more than 155 million in 1780.[5] These expenses were paid in borrowed money that was raised by Director General of Finances Jacques Necker, a Protestant banker with extensive contacts in the Netherlands, Switzerland, and other Protestant countries. He was forced, however, to pay exorbitant interest rates and to resort to dubious and expensive expedients like transferable annuities.[6] It was Necker's amazing ability to raise money that lay behind France's unprecedented war effort. From 1778 through 1782 French annual naval and colonial expenditures averaged about the same as the British navy's £6,720,000, equivalent about 160 million livres. In the previous war Britain's annual naval expenditure had been more than three times that of France. The French army spent almost as much as the French navy.[7]

Eventually Necker grew frightened at the war's cost and urged peace, thereby threatening American independence. He was particularly irate at Sartine's propensity for exceeding authorized spending. Meanwhile, the public blamed Sartine for how little the navy had accomplished for the vast sums it had spent. Spain, too, blamed Sartine for the war's continuation. Reluctantly the king had to dismiss Sartine on October 13, 1780, although he gave him a large pension and named him comte d'Alby.[8] Sartine and Machault were the two greatest naval ministers of the century, and both were sacrificed to French public opinion.

The harmony within the council of state disappeared. Sartine's replacement was Castries, the victor of Kloster Kamp, a supporter of Rochambeau, and a brilliant administrator. He, however, was a rival of Vergennes, who disagreed with him on war strategy. Castries believed that more of an effort should be made in India.[9] In late 1781 Maurepas died and Vergennes became his replacement as unofficial chief minister, but not until after the end of the war.[10] Necker overreached himself by seeking to gain admittance to the council of state. Louis XVI was remarkably tolerant of Protestants, eventually easing discrimination against them. But he was not prepared to have one in his council of state and so he dismissed Necker.

The problem of financing the war continued. The navy and colonies alone cost at least 162 million livres in 1781 and at least 200 million in 1782.[11] Even Vergennes grew frightened. In March 1781 he had Joseph-Mathias Gérard (now ennobled as Gérard de Rayneval) prepare a memoir on what the United States could afford to lose; Rayneval believed it could survive without Georgia and the Carolinas but not without New York. The following month Vergennes wrote his new minister plenipotentiary in Philadelphia that Louis might have to give up his commitment to American territorial integrity, but he would do so only in the last extremity.[12] The king increased his loans and grants to the United States during 1781, giving a 4 million livre loan and a 6 million livre gift, as well as guaranteeing a 10 million livre loan being raised in the Netherlands.[13] Louis's courage and perseverance were worthy of his ancestors Louis XIV and Louis XV, who had endured great crises seventy-five years and twenty years earlier.

Many in the United States also must have wondered if 1781 would be the last chance for victory. The soldiers of the Continental army long had been unpaid, ill clothed, and underfed.[14] At the beginning of 1781, the Pennsylvania Line (that state's contingent in the Continental army) mutinied. They marched out of the army's winter quarters of Morristown in the direction of Philadelphia. They did not defect to the British, and they agreed to meet with a joint committee of the Continental Congress and the Pennsylvania Supreme Executive Council. The meeting resolved one key issue: the soldiers' belief that their enlistments had expired. About half of the 2,400 Pennsylvania soldiers were given discharges. A revolt in the New Jersey Line was less well treated. Troops from West Point took 200 of the mutineers prisoner, and a few of them were put to death.[15]

The American Revolution was living on borrowed time. If the British had been cautious and not offered the allies a target, it is quite possible that the continuing French financial crisis would have broken the French will to continue fighting. The United States, totally dependent on French financial and naval assistance, would have been unable to continue without them. At best the United States to save its independence would have had to accept the loss of most or all of the territory Britain occupied, such as New York, Charleston, and Savannah.

That this did not happen was due to Cornwallis's mistaken strategy. To save South Carolina he invaded North Carolina. Washington's best subordinate, Nathanael Greene, now commanded the American Southern Army. He could not defeat Cornwallis, but he could inflict unacceptable casualties on them. Unsuccessful in North Carolina, Cornwallis marched to Virginia, where he established a base at Yorktown on the York River near Williamsburg so that he could remain in touch with Clinton at New York.[16] There the British navy could supply him, reinforce him, or evacuate him as long as they maintained control over the entrance to Chesapeake Bay. If the navy lost its superiority in numbers, however, Cornwallis's army would be as vulnerable as Burgoyne's had been, and an even more decisive American (and French) victory would be possible.

Possible Financial Collapse

EIGHTEEN

The Allies Might Not Have Achieved the Cooperation Needed for Victory

The campaign of 1781 would be decided by which side could bring the most ships of the line to bear at the key point. Just before the beginning of the year, Britain added a few ships of the line to its enemies' coalition. Since the beginning of the war, Britain had tried to deny the French navy access to masts, timber, copper, and naval stores from the Baltic Sea. The British navy brought into British ports neutral ships carrying such supplies and purchased them for itself. In February 1780 Empress Catherine II of Russia surprised the British by proclaiming Russia's right to carry naval stores to the belligerents and inviting other neutral countries to join a League of Armed Neutrality to protect the ships carrying them.[1] Sweden and Denmark, the other major Baltic powers, joined over the summer but were wary of defying the British navy.

The chief worry of the British government was that the Netherlands would join the League. The Dutch were major suppliers of the French navy, and through St. Eustatius and their other Caribbean islands they also provided provisions to the French West Indies and arms to the United States. The British feared that if the Dutch joined the League, they would obtain the help of the Baltic navies in sending masts and naval supplies to French ports like Brest. The British hope of weakening France by denying it access to naval supplies was an illusion. Except for a few items like copper and copper nails, the French dockyards were well stocked. Moreover the Dutch could ship masts through inland canals in the Austrian Netherlands to the Loire River of France.[2]

On November 20, 1780, the Estates General of the Netherlands voted to join the League. Before the Dutch representative in St. Petersburg could sign the agreement, the British opened hostilities. Catherine thereupon ruled that the Dutch were no longer neutral and hence could not join the League or receive its assistance.[3]

This was a serious mistake by Britain, even though the Dutch navy was small and unprepared for war; on April 1, 1781, only five Dutch ships of the line were at sea and another nine outfitting in port. By July, however, it was strong enough to threaten control of the North Sea, forcing the British to use ships and their crews to keep trade open. On August 5, 1781, six British ships of the line and a large frigate fought a similar Dutch squadron in the most ferocious battle of the war.[4] Equally important, the avaricious Rodney captured St. Eustatius as soon as he learned of the outbreak of the Dutch war and diverted part of his fleet to loading booty rather than fighting the French.

The Spaniards also helped, particularly by putting pressure on Gibraltar. On March 22 the British Home Fleet with its 28 ships of the line was off Cork, Ireland, to pick up provision ships for Gibraltar when a huge French fleet and convoy sailed unimpeded from Brest. Escorting more than 150 supply ships and transports were 20 ships of the line bound for Martinique, 5 for the Indian Ocean, and 1 for Boston.[5] Before the great fleet sailed, Castries met with the commander of the ships going to Martinique, Admiral François-Joseph-Paul, comte de Grasse. By an extraordinary piece of luck, Castries on his journey from the French court had met at Lorient Colonel John Laurens, an envoy from George Washington en route to beg the French court's help for Washington's army.[6] It is

Cooperation Needed for Victory

almost certain that Castries informed de Grasse of the dire condition of the Continental army. De Grasse would bring it an extraordinary amount of help when he left the Caribbean at the onset of the hurricane season.

De Grasse's assistance was only one part of what would be necessary to trap and capture Cornwallis at Yorktown. Rochambeau and Washington needed to cooperate in running the risk of bypassing the huge British garrison at New York without being attacked. The French, Spanish, and Dutch navies needed to put enough pressure on the British Home Fleet to prevent its sending numerous ships of the line to reinforce New York. Spain had to release the French troops at St. Domingue loaned for its use. Finally the French squadron at Newport had to bring siege artillery to Yorktown without being intercepted.[7] Amazingly, all these things happened and American independence was saved. For the generals and admirals of France, Spain, the United States, and the Netherlands to work together for the common good was unique in the history of eighteenth-century alliances. It was probably the greatest miracle to contribute to the miracle of American independence.

After seeing off the other portions of the great fleet, de Grasse reached Martinique on May 6.[8] With the ships he found already there he initially had an advantage of twenty-four ships of the line against eighteen British because Rodney had retained four ships of the line at St. Eustatius. (The convoy carrying Rodney's booty later was captured by a French squadron while en route to England, a splendid example of poetic justice.) De Grasse was able to capture the island of Tobago before sailing in July to St. Domingue (now Haiti).

There he met a French frigate bringing pilots for the American coast, as he had requested via the ship escorting the convoy for Boston.[9] The frigate also carried intelligence from Rochambeau, from the French minister in Philadelphia, and from Admiral Louis de Barras-Saint-Laurent, the commander of the squadron at Newport. They reported that Cornwallis and 6,000 troops were in Virginia and that Washington and Rochambeau planned to probe the defenses of New York. Washington and Rochambeau had agreed at a recent conference in Wethersfield, Connecticut, to request de Grasse to sail to New York. Rochambeau changed his mind and now recommended that de Grasse sail to the Chesapeake, but leaving him the choice. De Grasse chose to sail to Chesapeake Bay.

At St. Domingue de Grasse embarked 3,300 troops. He needed Spanish approval because some of the troops were intended for the use of Spain. The decision was the responsibility of Louisiana governor Bernardo de Gálvez, the superb general who recently had captured Pensacola with the help of a small French squadron that now joined de Grasse. Aboard one of the French ships was Gálvez's representative, Francisco Saavedra.[10] Not only did Saavedra release the troops but the people of Havana raised 1 million livres to pay Rochambeau's army (which de Grasse picked up at Matanzas, Cuba, en route to America). De Grasse brought all but one of his twenty-nine ships of the line with him, while Rodney sent to New York only fourteen of his twenty when he returned to England for his health. The British detachment was commanded by Samuel Hood, who was junior in seniority to Thomas Graves, commander of the squadron already at New York.

After a twenty-five-day passage from St. Domingue, de Grasse reached the entrance to Chesapeake Bay on August 30, the day before Graves and Hood sailed for Chesapeake Bay from New York, bringing with them nineteen ships of the line and a 50-gun ship. Washington and Rochambeau, who had been reconnoitering the defenses of New York, had learned on August 14 that de Grasse was en route to Chesapeake Bay. They decided to join him. On August 19, 3,000 Continental soldiers and 4,000 French troops began the long march to Virginia. By August 30 the army was west of

Staten Island. Clinton, still fearing an attack on New York, did not move to intercept them.

On September 5 a French frigate cruising off Cape Henry, the southern tip of the entrance to Chesapeake Bay, spotted Graves and Hood's approaching fleet. De Grasse left four ships of the line behind and left the bay with twenty-four ships of the line. The two components of the British fleet were unfamiliar with each other, Graves's signals were misinterpreted by Hood, and Hood refused to take any initiative; the ensuing battle ended in a draw.[11] For several days the rival fleets maneuvered unsuccessfully to gain an advantageous position for renewing the battle. This gave Barras the opportunity to enter the bay with his seven ships of the line, bringing with him the provisions and siege artillery needed to capture Cornwallis. On September 11 de Grasse reentered Chesapeake Bay while Graves and Hood returned to New York.

The siege of Yorktown began on September 20. Eventually Cornwallis's 7,200 troops were besieged by 5,800 Continental army soldiers, 3,000 Virginia militiamen, and 7,800 French troops, including those brought by de Grasse. It took them almost a month to surround and bombard Cornwallis's trapped army, which finally laid down its arms on October 19; the allied army and its prisoners had to be dispersed in order to find enough food. (Luckily de Grasse helped relieve the food shortage by sailing for the Caribbean on November 4.)[12] On the very day of Cornwallis's surrender, Graves and Hood, having repaired their damaged ships as best they could, sailed again for Virginia. They finally had received reinforcements from England, but they consisted of only three ships of the line. After they learned of the surrender, they returned to New York.

With Britain's last strike force in America in peril, why could more ships not be spared for America? Admittedly the British navy was outnumbered in 1781. On April 1 the British had ninety-four ships of the line and 50-gun ships in service compared with seventy French, fifty-four Spanish, and fourteen Dutch.[13] (The United States had only one ship of the line, which was still under construction.) The disparity was less serious than it appeared. The Spanish contingent in particular had too few sailors to make its ships close to equal in a fight. What was important was that every navy helped apply pressure, much as Grant used every American army to apply pressure on the Confederates in 1864. The Dutch fought magnificently, but the key component was the force of nineteen French and thirty Spanish ships of the line in the western approaches to the British Isles. The rival Home Fleet of twenty-one ships of the line retreated to Torbay on the south coast of England and was effectively rendered useless. Meanwhile a Spanish squadron escorted an army that invaded and eventually captured Minorca.[14]

The Battle of Yorktown dealt a mortal blow to Lord North's government, although its demise was not immediate. On March 4, 1782, the House of Commons passed a resolution that those advising or trying to prosecute offensive war in America were enemies of their country; sixteen days later North submitted his resignation. Ten days later the new British government ordered New York, Charleston, and Savannah evacuated and the troops sent to Halifax and the West Indies to carry on the fight against France and Spain.[15]

In September 1781 the British army in America had more than 35,000 effectives (plus another 9,000 in Canada) of which only a fifth were with Cornwallis.[16] Why did the loss of Cornwallis's army prove a fatal wound?

The answer largely was the impatience of the British electorate, which had for so long paid so much in taxes for such little result. It was not only willing but enthusiastic about continuing the war against the treacherous French and Spaniards, but it had lost hope of defeating the Americans. The

Cooperation Needed for Victory

shape of the peace and the extent of America's borders would now be in the hands of the diplomats and statesmen as the fighting in America gradually wound down. American independence might yet prove hollow if the United States did not make a peace giving it a chance of growth and self-defense.

NINETEEN

The Peace Treaty Could Have Left the
United States Too Weak to Survive

The British government that replaced North's on March 27, 1782, was a fragile coalition nominally headed by First Lord of the Treasury the Marquess of Rockingham, who fifteen years earlier had led the short-lived government that repealed the Stamp Act. Its most powerful members were Secretary of State for Foreign Affairs Charles James Fox and Secretary of State for Home and Colonial Affairs William Fitzmaurice Petty, Earl of Shelburne, an old acquaintance of Benjamin Franklin. Franklin and Shelburne were good friends of Anne-Catherine de Ligniville d'Autricourt Helvétius, the widow of the great French philosopher Claude-Adrien Helvétius. On March 22 Franklin wrote to congratulate Shelburne on the return of Britain's goodwill to America and to thank him on Madame Helvétius's behalf for sending her a gift of gooseberry bushes.[1] This note, which was carried by a mutual friend of Shelburne and of Franklin's neighbor Anne-Louise Boivin d'Hardancourt Brillon de Jouy,[2] gave Shelburne an excuse to begin the negotiations on which the future of American independence depended.[3]

When Shelburne received Franklin's note on April 5, he immediately moved to get the jump on his rival, Fox, who disputed with him the right to negotiate with the Americans. On April 14 Franklin was surprised by a visit from an emissary from Shelburne named Richard Oswald, an elderly Scottish friend of former president of Congress Henry Laurens.[4] He presented letters of introduction from Shelburne and Laurens, indicated that his visit was unofficial, and offered as his personal opinion (actually Shelburne's) that the United States should negotiate a separate peace (contrary to the terms of the Franco-American alliance) and should recommend to France that it not make excessive demands of Britain. Franklin replied that he could do nothing without consulting Vergennes and took Oswald to meet him. Oswald returned to London five days later, impressed by Franklin's sincerity and cordiality, although he found him taciturn.

For the moment Franklin was the sole representative of the United States in France. The previous year Congress, under French pressure, had revoked Adams's commission to negotiate peace and had replaced him with a five-member peace commission consisting of Adams, Franklin, Minister Designate to the Netherlands Laurens, Minister Designate to Spain John Jay, and former Virginia governor Thomas Jefferson. At the moment Adams was in the Netherlands negotiating Dutch recognition of the United States, Jay was in Spain, Laurens, who had been captured at sea, was on parole in London, and Jefferson, in mourning for his late wife, had chosen not to serve. The only member initially to accept Franklin's summons to Paris was John Jay, who arrived on June 23 but was quickly incapacitated by a European-wide influenza epidemic (that killed Rockingham on July 1).

Just before Oswald left for England, Franklin showed him a memorandum he had drafted. It suggested that if Britain wished not only peace but a real reconciliation with America, it should cede Canada to the United States; this could produce a revenue sufficient for the United States to reimburse Loyalists for the loss of their estates as well as frontiersmen whose homes had been burned. Foolishly he let Oswald make a copy. Had Shelburne wished to make the note public, he could have destroyed the reputation of Franklin with the French government and with Congress, which had given Franklin no authority to make concessions to the Loyalists and which had ordered the peace commissioners to consult the French and follow their wishes during the negotiations.[5] Shelburne kept the note secret, but Franklin had raised false expectations that Congress would compensate the Loyalists.

Oswald returned to Paris on May 4, followed three days later by Fox's representative Thomas Grenville, son of the prime minister responsible for the Stamp Act. Franklin, who described Grenville as a very sensible young gentleman, took him to meet Vergennes, with whom Fox had authorized him to negotiate. Grenville indicated to Franklin that he was willing to negotiate with him as well. Franklin thus was placed in the enviable position of being able to choose between Shelburne's representative and Fox's. Both wanted the same terms, as Grenville explained to Vergennes: a treaty recognizing American independence, but accompanied by France and Spain returning all their conquests to Britain (now including West Florida and Minorca, captured by Spain, and a chain of islands in the Caribbean, captured by France). Fox, however, differed from Shelburne in being willing to recognize American independence *prior* to discussion of other points.

Franklin was too subtle a negotiator to play off Fox against Shelburne. He had a more complex game to play, that of negotiating a separate treaty with Britain while publicly proclaiming his unwillingness to negotiate apart from France, on whom the United States was still economically dependent. According to Grenville, Franklin promised he would intervene with France on Britain's behalf. Oswald claimed that Franklin was disposed to peace even without the concurrence of France and much more without Spanish and Dutch concurrence. Later that month Vergennes told Franklin that France did not intend to negotiate on America's behalf; the king wished the United States and France's other allies to negotiate for themselves. All he required was that they sign their treaties on the same day.[6] Franklin later would abuse this trust by signing a separate agreement that was conditional on the other powers also reaching agreement, at which time a formal treaty could be signed. This condition was deceptive because American public opinion didn't understand the nature of the conditional agreement and would not have supported a continuation of the war effort for the benefit of America's allies.

Oswald was back in London for further consultations during the second half of May. By mid-June Franklin faced the decision of choosing the negotiator with whom he should deal, Grenville having returned with full powers to treat with any foreign power. On June 27 he chose Oswald, whom he described as "plain and sincere" with "no Desire but that of being Useful in doing Good," a misreading of the tough, shrewd, and nationalistic Oswald.[7] Franklin may have been more cunning than he appeared in picking Shelburne's representative over Fox's, even though Fox was prepared to offer immediate recognition of American independence. Fox had overreached himself with the king and with his fellow cabinet ministers, who on June 30 rejected his peace plan. Fox responded by announcing his intention to resign. The following day Rockingham died of influenza, and soon thereafter Shelburne became prime minister. He picked a relative lightweight, Thomas Robinson, Baron Grantham, as foreign secretary, but oversaw the American negotiations himself.[8] He retained Oswald to negotiate with the Americans until late October, when Undersecretary Henry Stachey came to Paris to assist him. The brilliant diplomat Alleyne Fitzherbert was appointed to negotiate with the French, Spaniards, and Dutch.[9]

Shelburne's defeat of Fox was vitally important. Fox was strongly anti-French and wished to recognize American independence so as to split the anti-British alliance and take revenge on France, Spain, and the Netherlands. He had no interest in granting the United States favorable terms on its borders with Florida and Canada or on its access to the New-foundland fishery. Shelburne was not a profound or systematic thinker, but his views on foreign policy were far more enlightened than were Fox's.[10] He was a strong believer in maintaining a connection between Britain and America. He thus shared King George III's reluctance to concede American independence, a bond that not only helped him win the king's approval for his becoming prime minister but later helped him persuade the king to recognize American independence. Shelburne himself finally accepted American independence because he perceived that Britain would remain a great power as long as it maintained commercial relations with the United States. Although he would have preferred the connection to be a formal one, he correctly believed (as Turgot had) that even if the United States was independent, it would trade predominantly with its familiar partner Britain. Even more unusually Shelburne did not share the public's hatred of France and wished better relations. His protégé, Chancellor of the Exchequer William Pitt the younger (son of the Earl of Chatham), would make a commercial treaty with France a few years after he became prime minister in 1783 (and would be opposed to Russian expansionism).

Shelburne's freedom from anti-French and anti-American prejudices was invaluable for making peace with France and the United States. Particularly important to Americans was his willingness to surrender British claims to the area beyond the Appalachian Mountains bordered by the Great Lakes, the Mississippi River, and Florida.[11] He was willing to do so because he believed Britain would be able to trade with the area without having to bear the expenses of administering it, as it had between 1760 and 1775. Possession of this area was a key issue for the United States, second in importance only to recognition of its independence. The United States ultimately received it, not because of military conquest (Britain still held Detroit and Clark's forces were in terrible shape), or even because of the skill of American negotiators, but because nobody else really wanted it all that much. Shelburne didn't want it. Spain was enough interested in the area to send a small force from St. Louis to Fort St. Joseph in what is now Michigan to stake a claim. It was far less important to Charles III, however, than were Gibraltar, Minorca, East Florida, and West Florida. France would have preferred that it, as well as Canada, remain British in order to keep the United States dependent on France, but Vergennes had little interest in the area and no interest in France's obtaining any of it. Instead he was fearful that American claims to the area would jeopardize the American-British negotiations and prevent a general peace.

By now Vergennes was desperate for peace. France had planned to follow up Yorktown with a joint Franco-Spanish attack on Jamaica to gain an equivalent for Gibraltar. Instead, de Grasse was defeated by Rodney on April 12, 1782, at the Battle of the Saintes (a group of small islands off Guadeloupe near where the battle was fought). Moreover there was a rising danger of a war between the Russians and the Turks over Russian designs on the Crimea. Vergennes used Rayneval in a futile attempt to broker a compromise between John Jay, now recovered from influenza, and Spanish ambassador to France Pedro Pablo Abarca de Bolea, conde de Aranda, so as to remove another obstacle to a general peace settlement. Jay misunderstood Vergennes's intentions as being anti-American.[12]

The key turning point in Franklin's negotiations came soon after Shelburne became first lord of the treasury. On July 10 Shelburne hinted to the House of Lords that Britain might have to concede American independence. On the same day Franklin read to Oswald his list of necessary (non-negotiable) American demands: (1) full and complete independence with the withdrawal of all British troops, (2) a border settlement with the British colonies (Canada and

Florida), (3) the restriction of Canada to, at most, those borders preceding the Quebec Act, and (4) American access to the Newfoundland fishery for both whaling and fishing. He also suggested some advisable articles that were not seriously discussed, such as an indemnity for American war victims, an apology from Great Britain for the distress it had caused, permission for American ships to trade in British and Irish ports as if they were British, and the relinquishing of Canada to the United States.[13]

Franklin did not have long to wait. On July 27 Shelburne informed Oswald that he would be sent a commission to conclude a peace treaty on the basis of Franklin's necessary articles.[14] With victory seemingly at hand, Franklin became so ill with kidney or bladder stones that he feared for his life.[15] John Jay took over the negotiations and nearly seized defeat from the jaws of victory. Although Jay would come to have a brilliant judicial and political career, his self-righteousness, arrogance, ignorance, and impatience set back the negotiations for a critical six weeks (August 15–September 27, 1782) during which the British beat back an attack on Gibraltar, undercutting Shelburne's quest for peace. Jay objected to the commission Shelburne sent Oswald because it referred to the "thirteen colonies" rather than the United States. Jay finally panicked and accepted a large meaningless compromise wording that the British could have rescinded had peace negotiations failed.[16]

What caused Jay to panic was his learning that Vergennes had sent Rayneval to Bowood, Shelburne's country estate. As usual Jay misunderstood, believing the trip an anti-American plot. Rayneval's mission really was to revive the stalled British-French negotiations; the American-British negotiations were discussed only in passing.[17] The initiative for the meeting was Shelburne's. He had sent back to France Admiral de Grasse, who had been taken prisoner at the Battle of the Saintes. De Grasse, who had been treated as a celebrity while in England, brought back Shelburne's promise of generous terms for all of Britain's opponents. Vergennes had ordered Rayneval to return to France if Shelburne withdrew his offer, but Shelburne so won his trust that he violated his instructions. Shelburne told him that during his tenure as secretary of state for the Southern Department (August 1766–October 1768) he had wished to cooperate with France against Russia and Prussia and prevent the partition of Poland. This appears to have been a fabrication, although he may have been a party to Rochford's 1773 secret discussions with the French. It did, however, convince Rayneval and later Vergennes that a peace settlement with Shelburne might lead to Britain's cooperating with France to save the Turks from Russia.[18]

The final American-British discussions for a conditional peace agreement began on October 1. Franklin had sufficiently regained his health to join Jay. At the end of the month John Adams, having signed a commercial treaty with the Netherlands, joined them. Even Laurens participated in the final day of discussions. Jay and Adams were suspicious that Franklin might defer to France's wishes, but the negotiations went smoothly. Indeed Franklin, still bitter at George III, was more adamant than his colleagues against concessions to the Loyalists. The commissioners did not obtain everything they might have, letting slip an opportunity to obtain the rich lands of what is now southern Ontario.[19] Moreover at Jay's insistence the treaty contained a secret supplemental article granting Britain a sizeable part of what is now Mississippi and Alabama if the British regained West Florida.[20] This was a despicable act of ingratitude to Spain, apparently motivated largely by Jay's spite for the poor treatment he had received during his abortive mission to Spain. It was also dangerous. If Britain had obtained either or both parts of Florida in the final peace treaty, it would have disastrously altered American history by making the abolition of slavery and defeat of the Confederacy much more difficult. Luckily Britain did not take up the offer.

On November 30 the four commissioners signed with Oswald a conditional peace agreement that would not take effect until Britain reached agreement with its other opponents.[21] This was a violation in spirit if not in letter of Congress's instructions not to make an agreement without the consent of France. These instructions had been forced on Congress, which was totally dependent on French military and financial assistance. The commissioners' violating them was nearly disastrous for France.[22] France, with enormous difficulty, had arranged a complex agreement to satisfy Spain by which Britain would receive French Guadeloupe and Spanish Minorca in exchange for Spain's receiving Gibraltar. France in turn would receive Spanish Santo Domingo (today's Dominican Republic) in compensation.

Outraged at the concessions to the United States, the British public was not willing to give up Gibraltar. There was a real danger that France's and Spain's negotiations with Britain would collapse, voiding America's conditional agreement. If war continued, the French and Spanish navies almost surely would be crushed; their finances were shaky, their ships needed repair, and they were critically short of sailors and officers. Admiral d'Estaing had been named commander of a huge Franco-Spanish fleet ordered to sail from Cadiz for another attempt at capturing Jamaica. Vergennes ordered him to meet with Charles III while en route in order to obtain permission to delay its sailing. Peace finally was saved by Ambassador Aranda, one of the greatest diplomats and statesmen of the eighteenth century. On his own authority he agreed on December 16 to accept Minorca, West Florida, and East Florida for Spain in lieu of Gibraltar. (East Florida was in exchange for the Bahamas, recently captured by Spain with the aid of a frigate from the South Carolina navy.)[23]

Aranda's courageous decision came just in time to avert a

The Peace Treaty

Franco-American diplomatic crisis. An anguished Vergennes wrote Franklin on December 15 to complain of the commissioners' breach of faith. Franklin's response of the 17th apologized for his violation of etiquette (*bienséance*), hinted that America might drop out of the war (thereby freeing the British garrisons of New York and Charleston to attack the French West Indies), and reminded Vergennes of his request for a new loan! Aranda's action of the previous day probably was responsible for Vergennes sending a conciliatory response to this rudeness and even granting a new loan.[24]

Britain signed formal peace treaties with Spain, France, and the United States (and a preliminary agreement with the Netherlands) on January 20, 1783. The American agreement confirmed the terms of the conditional agreement that granted the United States recognition of its independence, extraordinarily generous borders, and even access to the fishery.[25] The chief danger to American independence now came not from outside the United States but from within.

3

The Way the United States Could Have Lost Its Independence

TWENTY

The American Union Might Not Have Lasted

The peace treaty was confirmed by the signing of a similar final peace treaty (minus the secret article) on September 3, 1783.[1] The United States now had a place among recognized sovereign nations. Its area was comparable to or superior to any European country but Russia. Its population of 3 million (4 million by 1790)[2] was small by the standard of European great powers, but growing at an unparalleled rate because of the abundance of land taken from Native Americans. Famine was unknown, and except for slaves and Native Americans, its standard of living was the highest in the world. Although it had no large cities and little industry, it possessed abundant natural resources, a large merchant marine, acquisitive merchants, and industrious farmers unburdened by feudal institutions.[3] What it lacked in spite of the Articles of Confederation ratified in 1781 was a political system capable of guaranteeing its unity and protecting its independence.

Republics had a poor reputation in the eighteenth century.[4] They were either small and inconsequential (for example, the Republic of Ragusa) or populous but hamstrung by archaic political institutions (such as Poland). One of the most prominent republics was the United Provinces of the Netherlands, which was headed by an Estates General dependent on the unanimous consent of the estates of the seven Dutch provinces. The Continental Congress had a similar problem. Congress could fund itself by a common tax or set of customs duties only if all thirteen states consented. This proved to be impossible. Without money Congress could maintain only a token army and had to sell the remaining warships of the Continental navy, leaving American shipping to the Mediterranean prey to Barbary pirates.[5]

The euphoria of victory soon faded. Britain closed its Caribbean colonies to American shipping, and Spain closed the Mississippi River at New Orleans. Britain also refused to evacuate its posts in the Upper Country in retaliation for the American states refusing to compensate British creditors and Loyalists for their property losses.[6] Postwar economic difficulties and the decision to pay the government's debts, now mostly held by speculators, led to widespread social strife. Debtors in Massachusetts even seized law courts during the 1786 Shays' Rebellion.[7]

Congress did resolve the question of how to integrate the area west of the Appalachians into the union by authorizing the creation of new states. Relations among the existing states, however, were rancorous as they battled over trade and border disputes. American security was dependent on internal unity, but disputes within and among the states imperiled that unity. Many of the leading figures of the Revolution, such as Washington, James Madison, and Alexander Hamilton, were "nationalists" who believed that the American republic needed a strong central government for its stability and strength. Although humiliation at the hands of Britain, Spain, and the Barbary pirates reinforced their case, it was chiefly social conflict like Shays' Rebellion that provided the chief impetus for structural change. The Constitutional Convention of 1787 provided a new governmental framework that was supported by creditors and nationalists. The struggle for ratification was hard fought, but with its success and the unanimous election of Washington as president, American

The American Union

independence was safe, at least until the terrible threat of the Civil War. A new war with Britain in 1812 threatened American borders but not the independence of the United States.

Although American independence was marred by the continuing ill treatment of slaves and Native Americans, it gradually led to democratization, industrialization, and the development of a distinctive American culture. Had there been no revolution, America likely would have evolved like Canada in the same general direction. But had the revolution been defeated, America's fate, like that of Ireland or India, probably would have been far less benign. Thanks to the courage and sacrifice of the revolutionaries and the help of France, Spain, the Netherlands and America's Native American allies, American independence was secured and its social, political, and cultural life made free to evolve separately from Britain.

NOTES

1. America's Partial Autonomy

1. Daniel K. Richter, *Before the Revolution: America's Ancient Pasts* (Cambridge: Belknap Press of Harvard University Press, 2011), 327–45.

2. Geoffrey Parker, *Global Crisis: War, Climate Change, and Catastrophe in the Seventeenth Century* (New Haven: Yale University Press, 2013).

3. See, for example, Charles W. Ingrao, *The Habsburg Monarchy, 1648–1815*, 2nd ed. (Cambridge: Cambridge University Press, 1994), 139–40. See also Peter H. Wilson, "Poverty," in Wilson, ed., *A Companion to Eighteenth-Century Europe* (Milford MA: Blackwell, 2008), 110.

4. James A. Henretta, *"Salutary Neglect": Colonial Administration under the Duke of Newcastle* (Princeton: Princeton University Press, 1972).

5. Alan Tully, "The Political Development of the Colonies after the Glorious Revolution," in Jack P. Greene and J. R. Pole, eds., *A Companion to the American Revolution* (Medford MA: Blackwell, 2000), 29–38, provides an introduction. Jack P. Greene, *The Quest for Power: The Lower Houses of Assembly in the Southern Royal Colonies, 1680–1776* (Chapel Hill: University of North Carolina Press, 1963) is the classic work. For a brief description of how British colonial administration worked, see Ian K. Steele, "Metropolitan Administration of the Colonies, 1696–1775," in Greene and Pole, *Companion to the American Revolution*, 8–13.

6. Michael G. Kammen, *A Rope of Sand: The Colonial Agents, British Politics, and the American Revolution* (Ithaca NY: Cornell University Press, 1968).

7. Thomas P. Slaughter, *Independence: The Tangled Roots of the American Revolution* (New York: Hill and Wang, 2014); Alison G. Olson, "The Changing Socio-Economic and Strategic Importance of the

Colonies to the Empire," in Greene and Pole, *Companion to the American Revolution*, 19–28.

8. Jonathan R. Dull, *The Age of the Ship of the Line: The British and French Navies, 1650–1815* (Lincoln: University of Nebraska Press, 2009), 35–40. For the horrors of the previous centuries, see Lauro Martines, *Furies: War in Europe, 1450–1700* (New York: Bloomsbury Press, 2013).

9. Jeremy Black, *Natural and Necessary Enemies: Anglo-French Relations in the Eighteenth Century* (London: Duckworth, 1986). In 1707 the union of England and Scotland created a common government for Great Britain.

10. Dull, *Age of the Ship of the Line*, 39, 42; Brendan Simms, *Three Victories and a Defeat: The Rise and Fall of the First British Empire* (New York: Basic Books, 2008), 204–23.

11. Jeremy Black, *The Collapse of the Anglo-French Alliance, 1727–1731* (Gloucester UK: Alan Sutton; New York: St. Martin's Press, 1987); Arthur McCandliss Wilson, *French Foreign Policy during the Administration of Cardinal Fleury, 1726–1743: A Study in Diplomacy and Commercial Development* (Cambridge: Harvard University Press; London: Humphrey Milford, Oxford University Press, 1936).

12. John L. Sutton, *The King's Honor and the King's Cardinal: The War of the Polish Succession* (Lexington: University Press of Kentucky, 1980); Jeremy Black, "British Neutrality during the War of the Polish Succession," *International History Review* 8 (1986): 345–66.

13. Philip Woodfine, *Britannia's Glories: The Walpole Ministry and the 1739 War with Spain* (Woodbridge, Suffolk: Boydell Press for the Royal Historical Society, 1998); Richard Harding, *Amphibious Warfare in the Eighteenth Century: The British Expedition to the West Indies, 1740–1742* (Woodbridge: Boydell Press for the Royal Historical Society, 1991).

14. Reed Browning, *The War of the Austrian Succession* (New York: St. Martin's Press, 1993) and M. S. Anderson, *The War of the Austrian Succession, 1740–48* (London: Longman, 1995) are good introductions.

15. Francis Jennings, *The Ambiguous Iroquois Empire: The Covenant Chain Confederation of Indian Tribes with English Colonies from Its Beginnings to the Lancaster Treaty of 1744* (New York: W. W. Norton, 1984); Jon Parmenter and Mark Power Robison, "The Perils and Possibilities of Wartime Neutrality on the Edge of Empires: Iroquois and Acadians between the British and Acadians in North America, 1744–1760," *Diplomatic History* 31 (2007): 167–206; John Parmenter, "After the Mourning Wars: The Iroquois as Allies in Colonial North American Campaigns, 1675–1760," *William & Mary Quarterly*, 3rd. ser., 64 (2007): 39–82. The British colonists' fear and hatred of Native Amer-

icans has a large literature. Three books that particularly impressed me are John Grenier, *The First Way of War: American War Making on the Frontier, 1607-1814* (New York: Cambridge University Press, 2005), Peter Silver, *Our Savage Neighbors: How Indian War Transformed Early America* (New York: W. W. Norton, 2008), and James P. Merrell, *Into the American Woods: Negotiators on the Pennsylvania Frontier* (New York: W. W. Norton, 1999).

16. Jack M. Sosin, "Louisbourg and the Peace of Aix-la-Chapelle, 1748," *William & Mary Quarterly*, 3rd ser., 14 (1957): 516-35. For the importance of Louisbourg, see John Robert McNeill, *Atlantic Empires of France and Spain: Louisbourg and Havana, 1700-1763* (Chapel Hill: University of North Carolina Press, 1985).

17. Jack P. Greene, "Origins of the New Colonial Policy, 1748-1763," in Greene and Pole, *Companion to the American Revolution*, 101-11.

18. For the financing of Britain's wars, see John Brewer, *The Sinews of Power: War, Money, and the English State, 1688-1783* (New York: Alfred A. Knopf, 1989).

2. Colonial Rivalry of 1748-1755

1. The standard biography is Reed Browning, *The Duke of Newcastle* (New Haven: Yale University Press, 1975).

2. Jonathan R. Dull, *The French Navy and the Seven Years' War* (Lincoln: University of Nebraska Press, 2005), 4-9.

3. For the Acadians and their tragic fate, see N. G. S. Griffiths, *From Migrant to Acadian: A North American Border People, 1604-1755* (Montreal: McGill-Queen's University Press, 2008), Geoffrey Plank, *An Unsettled Conquest: The British Campaign against the People of Acadia* (Philadelphia: University of Pennsylvania Press, 2001), and Mack Farragher, *"A Great and Noble Scheme": The Tragic Story of the Expulsion of the Acadians from Their American Homeland* (New York: W. W. Norton, 2008). For a less sympathetic portrayal of the Acadians, see John Grenier, *The Far Reaches of Empire: War in Nova Scotia, 1710-1760* (Norman: University of Oklahoma Press, 2008).

4. There are numerous studies of the Franco-British colonial rivalry. A concise summary is in Daniel Baugh, *The Global Seven Years' War, 1754-1763: Britain and France in a Great Power Contest* (Harlow UK: Pearson Longman, 2011), 46-66. For the Native Americans of the Ohio Country, see Richard White, *The Middle Ground: Indians, Empires, and Republics in the Great Lakes Region, 1650-1815* (New York: Cambridge University Press, 1991), Michael N. McConnell, *A Country Between: The Upper Ohio Valley and Its People, 1724-1774* (Lincoln: University of Nebraska Press, 1992), and Eric Hindraker, *Elusive Empires: Con-*

structing Colonialism in the Ohio Valley, 1673-1800 (Cambridge: Cambridge University Press, 1997).

5. Enid Robbie, *The Forgotten Commissioner: Sir William Mildmay and the Anglo-French Commission of 1750-1755* (East Lansing: Michigan State University Press, 2003).

6. Dull, *French Navy and the Seven Years' War*, 20-28.

7. See Jeremy Black, *George II: Puppet of the Politicians?* (Exeter: Exeter University Press, 2007) and Andrew C. Thompson, *George II, King and Elector* (New Haven: Yale University Press, 2011).

8. Fred Anderson, *Crucible of War: The Seven Years' War and the Fate of Empire in British North America, 1754-1766* (New York: Alfred A. Knopf, 2000), 5-7, 45-65; D. Peter MacLeod, *The Canadian Iroquois and the Seven Years' War* (Toronto: Dundurn Press, 1996), 42-50.

9. See David Bell, "Jumonville's Death: Propaganda and National Identity in Eighteenth-Century France," in Colin Jones and Dror Wahrman, eds., *The Age of Cultural Revolution: Britain and France, 1750-1820* (Berkeley: University of California Press, 2002), 33-61, and John Shovlin, "Selling American Empire on the Eve of the Seven Years' War," *Past and Present* 206 (February 2010): 121-49.

10. The best account of the negotiations is T. R. Clayton, "The Duke of Newcastle, the Earl of Halifax, and the American Origins of the Seven Years' War," *Historical Journal* 24 (1981): 571-603.

11. Black, *Natural and Necessary Enemies*, 52.

12. Dull, *French Navy and the Seven Years' War*, 11-12; James Pritchard, *Louis XV's Navy, 1748-1762: A Study of Organization and Administration* (Montreal: McGill-Queen's University Press, 1987), 137-40.

3. The War of 1755

1. For the following discussion of British objectives for the 1755 campaign, see Clayton, "Duke of Newcastle," and Baugh, *Global Seven Years' War*, 79-91.

2. For the Albany conference, see Timothy Shannon, *Indians and Colonists at the Crossroad of Empire: The Albany Conference of 1754* (Ithaca: Cornell University Press, 2000), and Alison Gilbert Olson, "The British Government and Colonial Unity, 1754," *William & Mary Quarterly*, 3rd ser., 17 (1960): 22-34.

3. Dull, *French Navy and the Seven Years' War*, 25-26, 29-30, 262; Robert B. Wells, "Population and Family in Early America," in Greene and Pole, *Companion to the American Revolution*, 41.

4. Dull, *French Navy and the Seven Years' War*, 30-32; Baugh, *Global Seven Years' War*, 112-15.

5. Farragher, *"Great and Noble Scheme,"* 335–415, 424–25, 468–73; Plank, *Unsettled Conquest*, 140–57.

6. Paul P. Kopperman, *Braddock at the Monongahela* (Pittsburgh: University of Pittsburgh Press, 1977); Charles Hamilton, ed., *Braddock's Defeat: The Journal of Captain Robert Cholmley's Batman, the Journal of a British Officer, Halkett's Orderly Book* (Norman: University of Oklahoma Press, 1959); Thomas E. Crocker, *Braddock's March: How a Man Sent to Seize a Continent Changed American History* (Westholm UK: Yardley, 2009).

7. Matthew C. Ward, *Breaking the Backcountry: The Seven Years' War in Virginia and Pennsylvania, 1754-1763* (Pittsburgh: University of Pittsburgh Press, 2003); Merrell, *Into the American Woods*, 225–36; Jane T. Merritt, *At the Crossroads: Indians and Empires on the Mid-Atlantic Frontier, 1700-1763* (Chapel Hill: University of North Carolina Press, 2003), 169–97.

8. Francess G. Halpenny, ed., *Dictionary of Canadian Biography*, vol. 4, *1771 to 1800* (Toronto: University of Toronto Press; Quebec: Les Presses de l'Université Laval, 1979), 662–74; Roger Michalon, "Vaudreuil et Montcalm: Les Hommes, leurs relations, influence de ces relations sur la conduite de la guerre," in Jean Delmas et al., *Conflits des sociétés au Canada français pendant la guerre de Sept Ans et leur influence sur les operations: Colloque international de histoire militaire, Ottawa, 19-27 août, 1978* (Vincennes, France: Service historique de l'armée de terre, 1978), 41–140; Guy Frégault, *La Grand Marquis, Pierre de Rigaud de Vaudreuil et la Louisiane* (Montreal: Fides, 1952).

9. John Schutz, *William Shirley: King's Governor of Massachusetts* (Chapel Hill: University of North Carolina Press, 1961), 205–24. There are numerous biographies of Johnson. A recent one is Fintan O'Toole, *White Savage: William Johnson and the Invention of America* (London: Faber and Faber, 2005).

10. MacLeod, *Canadian Iroquois and the Seven Years' War*, 61–78; Russell P. Bellico, *Empires in the Mountains: French and Indian War Campaigns and Forts in the Lake Champlain, Lake George, and Hudson River Corridor* (Fleischmanns NY: Purple Mountain Press, 2010), 45–70.

11. Barry M. Moody, "'Delivered from all your distresses': The Fall of Quebec and the Remaking of Nova Scotia," in Phillip Buckner and John G. Reid, eds., *Revisiting 1759: The Conquest of Canada in Historical Perspective* (Toronto: University of Toronto Press, 2012), 218–40.

12. Michalon, "Vaudreuil et Montcalm" is an astute appraisal. For Montcalm see Halpenny, ed., *Dictionary of Canadian Biography*, vol.

3, *1741 to 1770* (Toronto: University of Toronto Press; Quebec: Les Presses de l'Université Laval, 1974), 458-69.

13. MacLeod, *Canadian Iroquois*, 79-94, and two articles by him, "The French Siege of Oswego in 1756: Inland Naval Warfare in North America," *American Neptune* 49 (1998): 262-71, and "The Canadians against the French: The Struggle for Control of the Expedition to Oswego in 1756," *Ontario History* 80 (1988): 143-57.

14. Stanley McCrory Pargellis, *Lord Loudoun* (New Haven: Yale University Press; London: Humphrey Milford, Oxford University Press, 1933). For the tension between the British army and the American colonists, see Alan Rogers, *Empire and Liberty: American Resistance to British Authority, 1755-1763* (Berkeley: University of California Press, 1974) and Douglas Edward Leach, *Roots of Conflict: British Armed Forces in Colonial America, 1677-1763* (Chapel Hill: University of North Carolina Press, 1986).

15. Dull, *French Navy and the Seven Years' War*, 38-39; Baugh, *Global Seven Years War*, 115-16, 142-46; T. J. A. LeGoff, "Problèmes de recrutement de la marine française pendant la Guerre de Sept Ans," *Revue Historique* 283 (January–June 1990), 205-33; Jacques Aman, *Une campagne navale méconnue à la vielle de la guerre de Sept Ans: L'Escadre de Brest en 1755* (Versailles: Service historique de la marine, 1986).

4. France Could Have Won the War

1. For the following analysis, see Dull, *French Navy and the Seven Years' War*, 36-37.

2. In this, France was successful: Johannes Burckhardt, "Religious War or Imperial War? Views of the Seven Years' War from Germany and Rome," in Mark H. Danley and Patrick J. Speelman, eds., *The Seven Years' War: Global Views* (Leiden: Brill, 2012), 107-33.

3. Dull, *French Navy and the Seven Years' War*, 38-39, 42-46, 49.

4. David Bayne Horn, *Sir Charles Hanbury Williams and European Diplomacy (1747-58)* (London: G. C. Harrap, 1930) and "The Duke of Newcastle and the Origins of the Diplomatic Revolution," in J. H. Elliot and H. G. Koenigsberger, eds., *The Diversity of History: Essays in Honor of Sir Herbert Butterfield* (Ithaca: Cornell University Press, 1970), 245-68. For Empress Elizabeth, see Eugeny V. Ansimov, *Empress Elizabeth: Her Reign and Her Russia, 1741-1761*, trans. John T. Alexander (Gulf Breeze FL: Academic International Press, 1995). There are two capable published doctoral dissertations on British-Prussian relations during the war: Patrick Doran, *Andrew Mitchell and Anglo-Prussian Diplomatic Relations during the Seven Years' War* (New York: Garland, 1986) and Karl W. Schweizer, *Frederick the Great, William*

Pitt, and Lord Bute: The Anglo-Prussian Alliance, 1756-1763 (New York: Garland, 1991). Later versions of Schweizer's work bear different titles.

5. See Herbert H. Kaplan, *Russia and the Outbreak of the Seven Years' War* (Berkeley: University of California Press, 1968).

6. For the Minorca campaign, see Dudley Pope, *At Twelve Mr. Byng Was Shot* (Philadelphia: J. P. Lippincott, 1962), Chris Ware, *Admiral Byng: His Rise and Execution* (Barnsley UK: Pen and Sword, 2009), and Sir Herbert W. Richmond, ed., *Papers Relating to the Loss of Minorca in 1756* (London: Naval Records Society, 1913).

7. Richard Harding, *The Emergence of Britain's Global Supremacy: The War of 1739-1748* (Woodbridge, Suffolk: Boydell and Brewer, 2010), 287. For a summary of Anson's achievements at the Admiralty, see Richard Middleton, "Naval Administration in the Age of Pitt and Anson," in Jeremy Black and Philip Woodfine, eds., *The British Navy and the Use of Sea Power in the Eighteenth Century* (Atlantic Highlands NJ: Humanities Press International, 1989), 109-27.

8. Unless otherwise noted, totals of ships of the line will include 50-gun ships, which occasionally were used in a line of battle. The present ships and their locations on June 1, 1756, are listed in Dull, *French Navy and the Seven Years' War*, 263-65.

9. This interpretation was advanced in the memoirs of Abbé (later Cardinal) François-Joachim de Pierre de Bernis, the chief French negotiator. Bernis's veracity is challenged by Léon Cahen, "Les Mémoires du Cardinal de Bernis et les débuts de la guerre de Sept Ans," *Revue d'histoire moderne et contemporaine* 12 (1909): 73-99. My account in *French Navy and the Seven Years' War*, 64-67, agrees with Cahen. For a more traditional interpretation, see Baugh, *Global Seven Years' War*, 174-82.

10. Dull, *French Navy and the Seven Years' War*, 89-94.

11. In my opinion the best brief account of the war in Europe is Franz A. J. Szabo, *The Seven Years' War in Europe, 1756-1763* (Harlow UK: Pearson Longman, 2008). But see also Richard Waddington, *La Guerre de Sept Ans: Histoire diplomatique et militaire*, 5 vols. (Paris: Firmin-Didot, 1899-1914), Christopher Duffy, *Frederick the Great: A Military Life* (London: Routledge and Kegan Paul, 1985), and Dennis Showalter, *The Wars of Frederick the Great* (London: Longman, 1996).

12. Sir Reginald Savory, *His Britannic Majesty's Army in Germany during the Seven Years' War* (Oxford: Clarendon Press, 1966), 8-48.

13. Dull, *French Navy and the Seven Years' War*, 78-80, 266-68; A. J. B. Johnston, *Endgame 1758: The Promise, the Glory, and the Despair of Louisbourg's Last Decade* (Lincoln: University of Nebraska Press,

2007), 115-47; Hugh Boscawen, *The Capture of Louisbourg, 1758* (Norman: University of Oklahoma Press, 2011), 40-41.

14. Ian K. Steele, *Betrayals: Fort William Henry and the "Massacre"* (New York: Oxford University Press, 1990) is the best account.

15. Christopher Duffy, *Prussia's Glory: Rossbach and Leuthen, 1757* (Chicago: Emperor's Press, 2003).

5. The American Frontier

1. Dull, *French Navy and the Seven Years' War*, 80-81, 105-9, 266-71. Boscawen, *The Capture of Louisbourg* and Johnston, *Endgame* provide the best accounts of the siege.

2. William R. Nestor, *The Epic Battle for Ticonderoga, 1758* (Albany: State University of New York Press, 2008); Rene Chartrand, *Ticonderoga, 1758: Montcalm's Victory against All Odds* (Westport CT: Praeger, 2000); Ian McCulloch, "'Like roaring lions breaking from their chains': The Battle of Ticonderoga, 8 July 1758," in Donald E. Graves, ed., *Fighting for Canada: Seven Battles, 1748-1945* (Toronto: Robin Brass Studio, 2000), 23-80.

3. Douglas R. Cubbison, *The British Defeat of the French in Pennsylvania, 1758: A Military History of the Forbes Campaign against Fort Duquesne* (Jefferson NC: McFarland, 2010).

4. Francis Jennings, *Empire of Fortune: Crowns, Colonies, and Tribes in the Seven Years' War in America* (New York: W. W. Norton, 1988), 253-404.

5. Dull, *French Navy and the Seven Years' War*, 148-49.

6. William G. Godfrey, *Pursuit of Profit and Preferment in Colonial North America: John Bradstreet's Quest* (Waterloo, Canada: Wilfrid Laurier University Press, 1982), 108-35.

7. For Pitt's key but collaborative role in British war strategy, see Richard Middleton, *The Bells of Victory: The Pitt-Newcastle Ministry and the Conduct of the Seven Years' War, 1757-1762* (Cambridge: Cambridge University Press, 1985).

8. Dull, *French Navy and the Seven Years' War*, 106-9, 142-43, 173-74; Jean Elizabeth Lunn, "Agriculture and War in Canada, 1740-1760," *Canadian Historical Review* 16 (1935): 123-36; Gilles Archambault, "La Question des vivres au Canada au cours de l'hiver 1757-1758," *Revue d'histoire de l'Amérique française* 21 (1967-68): 16-50; Jean de Maupassant, *Un Grand Armateur de Bordeaux, Abraham Gradis (1699?-1780)* (Bordeaux: Ferret et fils, 1917).

9. Dull, *French Navy and the Seven Years' War*, 41-42.

10. Among the many histories of the Quebec campaign are C. P. Stacey, *Quebec, 1759: The Siege and the Battle*, 2nd ed. (Toronto: Robin

Brass Studio, 2002); D. Peter MacLeod, *Northern Armageddon: The Battle of the Plains of Abraham* (Vancouver and Toronto: Douglas & McIntyre, 2008), Dan Snow, *The Battle of Quebec and the Birth of Empire* (London: Harper Press, 2009), and Matthew C. Ward, *The Battle for Quebec* (Stoud UK: Tempus, 2005). Buckner and Reid, *Revisiting 1759* has a number of interesting articles on the campaign.

11. See Erica Charters, "The Caring Fiscal-Military State during the Seven Years' War, 1756–1763," *Historical Journal* 52 (2009): 934.

12. John Shy, *Toward Lexington: The Role of the British Army in the Coming of the American Revolution* (Princeton: Princeton University Press, 1965) is the standard history of the British army in the American colonies. See also Peter D. G. Thomas, "The Grenville Program, 1763–1765," in Greene and Pole, *Companion to the American Revolution*, 118–22.

13. Colin Calloway, *The Scratch of a Pen: 1763 and the Transformation of North America* (Oxford: Oxford University Press, 2006); Gregory Evans Dowd, *War under Heaven: Pontiac, the Indian Nations, and the British Empire* (Baltimore: Johns Hopkins University Press, 2002); Richard Middleton, *Pontiac's War: Its Causes, Course, and Consequences* (New York: Routledge, 2007); David Dixon, *Never Come to Peace Again: Pontiac's Uprising and the Fate of the British Empire in North America* (Norman: University of Oklahoma Press, 2005); Keith R. Widder, *Beyond Pontiac's Shadow: Michilimackinac and the Anglo-Indian War of 1763* (East Lansing: Michigan State University Press; Mackinac Island: Mackinac State Historical Park, 2013).

14. Stephen Conway, "The Consequences of the Conquest: Quebec and British Politics, 1760–1774," Heather Welland, "Commercial Interest and Political Allegiance: The Origins of the Quebec Act," and Donald Fyson, "The Conquered and the Conqueror: The Mutual Adaptation of the *Canadiens* and the British in Quebec, 1759–1775," in Buckner and Reid, *Revisiting 1759*, 141–65, 166–89, 190–217; P. D. G. Thomas, *Tea Party to Independence: The Third Phase of the American Revolution, 1773–1776* (Oxford: Clarendon Press, 1991), 88–117.

15. For the economic difficulties, see Gary B. Nash, *The Urban Crucible: Social Change, Political Consciousness, and the Origins of the American Revolution* (Cambridge: Harvard University Press, 1979).

16. See Richard Archer, *As If an Enemy's Country: The British Occupation of Boston and the Origins of Revolution* (Oxford: Oxford University Press, 2010).

6. The Stamp Act Fiasco

1. See John Murrin, "The French and Indian War, the American Revolution, and the Counterfactual Hypothesis: Reflections on Lawrence

Henry Gipson and John Shy," *Reviews in American History* 1 (1973): 307–18, and Jack P. Greene, "The Seven Years' War and the American Revolution: The Causal Relation Reconsidered," *Journal of Imperial and Commonwealth History* 8 (1979–80): 85–105.

2. Thomas Truxes, *Defying Empire: Trading with the Enemy in Colonial New York* (New Haven: Yale University Press, 2008); Richard Pares, *War and Trade in the West Indies, 1739–1763* (Oxford: Clarendon Press, 1936) and *Yankees and Creoles: The Trade between North America and the West Indies before the American Revolution* (Cambridge: Harvard University Press, 1956).

3. For Grenville see Philip Lawson, *George Grenville: A Political Life* (Oxford: Clarendon Press, 1984).

4. Anderson, *Crucible of War*, 572–80 provides of a summary of the act.

5. Anderson, *Crucible of War*, 583–85.

6. Bernard Bailyn, *Faces of Revolution: Personalities and Themes in the Struggle for American Independence* (New York: Alfred A. Knopf, 1990), 83. For the growth in power of the British government, see Brewer, *Sinews of Power*.

7. See Bernard Bailyn, *The Ideological Origins of the American Revolution* (Cambridge: Harvard University Press, 1967).

8. I have discussed how American traits hindered its development as a naval power: Jonathan R. Dull, *American Naval History, 1607–1815: Overcoming the Colonial Legacy* (Lincoln: University of Nebraska Press, 2012).

9. Histories of the Stamp Act include P. D. G. Thomas, *British Politics and the Stamp Act Crisis: The First Phase of the American Revolution, 1763–1767* (Oxford: Clarendon Press, 1975), John L. Bullion, *A Great and Necessary Measure: George Grenville and the Genesis of the Stamp Act, 1763–1765* (Princeton: Princeton University Press, 1982), and Edmund S. and Helen M. Morgan, *The Stamp Act Crisis: Prologue to Revolution*, 2nd ed. (New York: Collier Books, 1963).

10. Peter D. G. Thomas, *George III, King and Politicians, 1760–1770* (Manchester: Manchester University Press, 2002), 114–20; Anderson, *Crucible of War*, 652–56; Paul Langford, *The First Rockingham Administration, 1765–1766* (Oxford: Oxford University Press, 1973).

11. Robert Middlekauff, *Benjamin Franklin and His Enemies* (Berkeley: University of California Press, 1996), 32–120; Leonard W. Labaree et al., eds., *The Papers of Benjamin Franklin*, 41 vols. to date (New Haven: Yale University Press, 1959–), 12:271–74. For Americans in London, see Julie Flavell, *When London Was Capital of America* (New Haven: Yale University Press, 2011).

12. Labaree, *Papers of Benjamin Franklin*, 13:124–62.

13. See Brendon McConville, *The King's Three Faces: The Rise and Fall of Royal America, 1688–1776* (Chapel Hill: University of North Carolina Press, 2006) for the changing attitudes about the king.

14. Thomas, *George III*, 125–47.

15. H. M. Scott, *British Foreign Policy in the Age of the American Revolution* (Oxford: Clarendon Press, 1990), 97–101; John Brooke, *The Chatham Administration, 1766–1768* (London: Macmillan, 1956); Sir Lewis Namier and John Brooke, *Charles Townshend* (New York: St. Martin's Press, 1964); P. D. G. Thomas, *The Townshend Duties Crisis: The Second Phase of the American Revolution, 1767–1773* (Oxford: Clarendon Press, 1987).

16. Alan Valentine, *Lord North*, 2 vols. (Norman: University of Oklahoma Press, 1967) is the fullest biography; for a brief sketch, see Andrew Jackson O'Shaughnessy, *The Men Who Lost America: British Leadership, the American Revolution, and the Fate of the Empire* (New Haven: Yale University Press, 2013), 47–79.

7. War with the American Colonies

1. Frederick V. Mills Sr., "Bishops and Other Ecclesiastical Issues to 1776," in Greene and Pole, *Companion to the American Revolution*, 179–83.

2. Labaree, *Papers of Benjamin Franklin*, 19:399–413; 20:268–86, 380–81, 513–16, 539–80; 21:5–9, 13–23, 31–34, 37–75, 85–96, 99–101, 197–202, 414–35.

3. Jesse Lemisch, "Jack Tar in the Streets: Merchant Seamen in the Politics of Revolutionary America," *William & Mary Quarterly*, 3rd ser., 25 (1968): 371–401; Neill R. Stout, *The Royal Navy in America, 1760–1775: A Study of Enforcement of British Colonial Policy in the Era of the American Revolution* (Annapolis: Naval Institute Press, 1973); Denver Brunsman, *The Evil Necessity: British Naval Impressment in the Eighteenth-Century Atlantic World* (Charlottesville: University Press of Virginia, 2013); Sarah Kinkel, "The King's Pirates? Naval Enforcement of Imperial Authority, 1740–76," *William & Mary Quarterly*, 3rd ser., 71 (2014): 3–34; David Lyon, *The Sailing Navy List: All the Ships of the Royal Navy—Built, Purchased, and Captured—1688–1860* (London: Conway Maritime Press, 1993), 211–12. Nick Bunker, *An Empire on the Edge: How Britain Came to Fight America* (New York: Alfred A. Knopf, 2014), a superb study of British-American relations between 1771 and 1775, discusses the terrible consequences of the incident.

4. Bernard Bailyn, *The Ordeal of Thomas Hutchinson* (Cambridge: Harvard University Press, 1974); Benjamin Woods Labaree, *The Bos-*

ton Tea Party (New York: Oxford University Press, 1964); Benjamin Carp, *The Boston Tea Party and the Making of America* (New Haven: Yale University Press, 2010).

5. David Ammerman, *In the Common Cause: American Response to the Coercive Acts of 1774* (Charlottesville: University Press of Virginia, 1974); T. H. Breen, *American Insurgents, American Patriots: The Revolution of the People* (New York: Hill and Wang, 2010); Richard D. Brown, *Revolutionary Politics in Massachusetts: The Boston Committee of Correspondence and the Towns, 1772-1774* (Cambridge: Harvard University Press, 1970); Robert A. Gross, *The Minutemen and Their World* (New York: Hill and Wang, 1976).

6. Bernard Donoughue, *British Politics and the Path to War, 1773-1775* (New York: St. Martin's Press, 1964); Charles R. Ritcheson, *British Politics and the American Revolution* (Norman: University of Oklahoma Press, 1954).

7. For the negotiations, see Labaree, *Papers of Benjamin Franklin*, 21:360-68, 372-73, 376-86, 408-11, 413, 444-45, 491-502, 514-15, 531-34, 540-99.

8. David Hackett Fischer, *Paul Revere's Ride* (New York: Oxford University Press, 1994).

8. American Resistance in 1775

1. R. Arthur Bowler, *Logistics and the Failure of the British Army in America, 1775-1783* (Princeton: Princeton University Press, 1975) discusses the feeding of the British army in America.

2. See Max M. Mintz, *The Generals of Saratoga: John Burgoyne and Horatio Gates* (New Haven: Yale University Press, 1990), Ira D. Gruber, *The Howe Brothers and the American Revolution* (New York: Atheneum, 1972), and William B. Willcox, *Portrait of a General: Sir Henry Clinton in the War of Independence* (New York: Alfred A. Knopf, 1964).

3. See Charles Royster, *A Revolutionary People at War: The Continental Army and American Character, 1771-1783* (Chapel Hill: University of North Carolina Press, 1979).

4. The expression "radical Loyalism" is that of the social historian Gary Nash; see his *Unknown American Revolution: The Unruly Birth of Democracy and the Struggle to Create America* (New York: Viking, 2005), 238-47. For the "rage militaire" and its eventual waning, see Royster, *Revolutionary People at War*.

5. John Ferling, *Almost a Miracle: The American Victory in the War of Independence* (New York: Oxford University Press, 2007) is a good military history of the war from an American perspective. Robert Mid-

dlekauff, *The Glorious Cause: The American Revolution, 1763-1789*, rev. ed. (New York: Oxford University Press, 2005) is a broader survey.

6. Nathaniel Philbrick, *Bunker Hill: A City, a Siege, a Revolution* (New York: Viking, 2013).

7. Jack N. Rakove, *The Beginnings of National Politics: An Interpretive History of the Continental Congress* (New York: Alfred A. Knopf, 1979) is the best history, although Edmund Cody Burnett, *The Continental Congress* (New York: Macmillan, 1941) and H. James Henderson, *Party Politics in the Continental Congress* (New York: McGraw-Hill, 1974) also are useful.

8. There are many biographies of Washington. The most thorough are Douglas Southall Freeman, John A. Carroll, and Mary W. Ashworth, *George Washington: A Biography*, 7 vols. (New York: Charles Scribner's Sons, 1948-57) and James Thomas Flexner, *George Washington*, 4 vols. (Boston: Little, Brown, 1965-72). Robert Middlekauff, *Washington's Revolution: The Making of America's First Leader* (New York: Knopf Doubleday, 2015) is an excellent introduction to his military career.

9. Labaree, *Papers of Benjamin Franklin*, 22:224-41, 274-77. For Franklin's military service, see J. Bennett Nolan, *General Benjamin Franklin: The Military Career of a Philosopher* (Philadelphia: University of Pennsylvania Press; London: Humphrey Milford, Oxford University Press, 1936).

10. James L. Nelson, *George Washington's Secret Navy: How the American Revolution Went to Sea* (New York: McGraw-Hill, 2008).

11. Dull, *American Naval History*, 17-32; William M. Fowler Jr., *Rebels under Sail: The American Navy during the Revolution* (New York: Charles Scribner's Sons, 1976).

12. Labaree, *Papers of Benjamin Franklin*, 22:310-18.

9. The French Navy

1. Dull, *French Navy and the Seven Years' War*, 151-63, 214, 243, 245.

2. Middleton, *Bells of Victory*, 183-84.

3. Dull, *French Navy and the Seven Years' War*, 14, 195-98.

4. Savory, *His Britannic Majesty's Army*, 203-78; Szabo, *Seven Years' War*, 300-305; Dull, *French Navy and the Seven Years' War*, 180-81, 275-77.

5. Middleton, *Bells of Victory*, 177-99; Dull, *French Navy and the Seven Years' War*, 187-211.

6. T. R. Ashton, *Economic Fluctuations in England, 1700-1800* (Oxford: Clarendon Press, 1959), 76, 150-51.

7. Patrick J. Speelman, "Strategic Illusions and the Iberian War of 1762," in Donley and Speelman, *Seven Years' War: Global Views*, 429–59.

8. Jeremy Black, *George III: America's Last King* (New Haven: Yale University Press, 2006) is an excellent biography. For the peace negotiations, see Dull, *French Navy and the Seven Years' War*, 228–44.

9. See P. J. Marshall, *The Making and Unmaking of Empires: Britain, India, and America, c. 1750–1783* (Oxford: Oxford University Press, 2005).

10. Paul W. Mapp, *The Elusive West and the Contest for Empire, 1713–1763* (Chapel Hill: University of North Carolina Press, 2011), 359–86.

11. Dull, *French Navy and the Seven Years' War*, 243.

12. Szabo, *Seven Years' War*, 430.

13. Christopher Clark, *Iron Kingdom: The Rise and Downfall of Prussia, 1600–1947* (Cambridge: Belknap Press of Harvard University Press, 2006), 210; Patrick Speelman, "Conclusion: Father of the Modern Age," in Donley and Speelman, *Seven Years' War: Global Views*, 523–27.

14. See David L. Preston, *The Texture of Contact: European and Indian Settler Communities on the Frontiers of Iroquoia, 1667–1783* (Lincoln: University of Nebraska Press, 2009).

10. The Pleas for Better Relations

1. Carol S. Leonard, *Reform and Regicide: The Reign of Peter III of Russia* (Bloomington: Indiana University Press, 1993); Isabel de Madariaga, *Russia in the Age of Catherine the Great* (New Haven: Yale University Press, 1981); Robert K. Massie, *Catherine the Great: Portrait of a Woman* (New York: Random House, 2011).

2. H. M. Scott, "Great Britain, Poland, and the Russian Alliance, 1763–1767," *Historical Journal* 19 (1976): 53–74, and *British Foreign Policy in the Age of the American Revolution*, 53–67; David Bayne Horn, "The Cabinet Controversy on Subsidy Treaties in Time of Peace, 1749–50," *English Historical Review* 45 (1930): 463–66; Reed Browning, "The Duke of Newcastle and the Imperial Election Plan, 1749–1754," *Journal of British Studies* 7 (1967): 28–47.

3. For a defense of this policy, see Michael Roberts, *Splendid Isolation, 1763–1780* (Reading: University of Reading, 1970).

4. Dull, *French Navy and the Seven Years' War*, 226, 245–49; H. M. Scott, "The Importance of Bourbon Naval Reconstruction to the Strategy of Choiseul after the Seven Years' War," *International History Review* 1 (1979): 17–35; Raymond E. Abarca, "Classical Diplomacy and Bourbon 'Revanche' Strategy, 1763–1770," *Review of Politics* 32 (1970): 326.

5. H. M. Scott, *The Emergence of the Eastern Powers, 1756-1775* (London: Cambridge University Press, 2001).

6. Dull, *French Navy and the Seven Years' War*, 7, 24-25, 44, 73, 128, 157-58, 168, 227, 238, 249-50; Michel Antoine and Didier Ozanam, "Le Secret du Roi et la Russie jusqu'à la morte de la czarina Elizabeth en 1762," *Annuaire-Bulletin de la Société de histoire de France* 86 (1954-55): 69-93.

7. For Vergennes and Sartine, see Orville T. Murphy, *Charles Gravier, Comte de Vergennes: French Diplomacy in the Age of Revolution, 1719-1787* (Albany: State University of New York Press, 1992) and Jacques Michel, *Du Paris de Louis XV à la marine de Louis XVI: L'œuvre de Monsieur de Sartine*, 2 vols. (Paris: Editions de l'érudit, 1982-84).

8. M. S. Anderson, "Great Britain and the Russian Fleet, 1769-70," *Slavonic and East European Review* 31 (1952-53): 148-63.

9. Scott, *British Foreign Policy in the Age of the American Revolution*, 115-22; Nicholas Tracy, *Navies, Deterrence, and American Independence: Britain and Seapower in the 1760s and 1770s* (Vancouver: University of British Columbia Press, 1988); Thad E. Hall, *France and the Eighteenth-Century Corsican Question* (New York: New York University Press, 1971); Geoffrey Rice, "Deceit and Distraction: Britain, France, and the Corsican Crisis of 1768," *International History Review* 28 (2006): 287-315.

10. Scott, *British Foreign Policy in the Age of the American Revolution*, 140-56; Dull, *French Navy and the Seven Years' War*, 247-48; H. M. Scott, "Choiseul et le troisième Pacte de Famille," in Lucien Bély, ed., *Le Présence des Bourbons en Europe XVIe-XXIe siecle* (Paris: Presses Universitaires de France, 2003), 207-20; Julius Goebel Jr., *The Struggle for the Falkland Islands: A Study in Legal and Diplomatic History* (New Haven: Yale University Press, 1927).

11. For d'Aiguillon as well as the struggle against the Parlements, see Lucien Laugier, *Une Ministére réformateur sous Louis XV: Le Triumverat (1770-1774)* (Paris: La Pensee universelle, 1975).

12. Herbert H. Kaplan, *The First Partition of Poland* (New York: Columbia University Press, 1962).

13. Quoted (with my translation) in Jonathan R. Dull, "France and the American Revolution Seen as Tragedy," in Ronald Hoffman and Peter J. Albert, eds., *Diplomacy and Revolution: The Franco-American Alliance of 1778* (Charlottesville: University Press of Virginia, 1981), 81n.

14. For the Swedish crisis and the failed French attempt at cooperation, see Scott, *British Foreign Policy in the Age of the American Revolution*, 181-91, Bunker, *Empire on the Edge*, 111-12, 128, 189-91, and

two great works by Michael Roberts, *British Diplomacy and Swedish Politics, 1758-1773* (Minneapolis: University of Minnesota Press, 1980) and "Great Britain and the Swedish Revolution, 1772-73," *Historical Journal 7* (1964): 1-46.

15. Albert Sorel, *Essais d'histoire et de critique*, 4th ed. (Paris: E. Plon, 1913), 178, quoted in Dull, *French Navy and the Seven Years' War*, 381. For the selection of Vergennes, see John Hardman, *Louis XVI* (New Haven: Yale University Press, 1993), 31-32, and *French Politics, 1774-1789: From the Accession of Louis XVI to the Fall of the Bastille* (London: Longman, 1995), 22, 34-36.

16. Jonathan R. Dull, *The French Navy and American Independence: A Study of Arms and Diplomacy, 1774-1787* (Princeton: Princeton University Press, 1975), 316-17, and "Vergennes, Rayneval, and the Diplomacy of Trust," in Ronald Hoffman and Peter J. Albert, eds., *Peace and the Peacemakers: The Treaty of 1783* (Charlottesville: University Press of Virginia, 1986), 131n.

17. Dull, *French Navy and the Seven Years' War*, 253-54; Ruth Strong Hudson, *The Minister from France: Conrad Alexandre Gérard, 1729-1790* (Euclid, Ohio: Lutz Printing, 1994).

18. Labaree, *Papers of Benjamin Franklin*, 22:310-12; Dull, *French Navy and American Independence*, 28-31.

11. Louis XVI Arms the Americans

1. Dull, *French Navy and American Independence*, 30-36, 76-77, 377.

2. Dull, *French Navy and American Independence*, 36-49. For Turgot and his reform program, see Douglas Dakin, *Turgot and the Ancien Regime in France* (London: Methuen, 1939).

3. See Brian N. Morton and Donald Spinelli, *Beaumarchais and the American Revolution* (Latham MD: Lexington Books, 2003).

4. Dull, *French Navy and American Independence*, 351-53, 359-60.

5. Thomas J. Schaeper, *Edward Bancroft: Scientist, Author, Spy* (New Haven: Yale University Press, 2011).

6. Kevin Phillips, *1775: A Good Year for Revolution* (New York: Viking, 2012), 431-45.

7. For suspicion of France, see James H. Hutson, "The Partition Treaty and the Declaration of Independence," *Journal of American History* 58 (1971-72): 877-96. Among the books about the Declaration are Pauline Maier, *American Scripture: Making the Declaration of Independence* (New York: Alfred A. Knopf, 1997) and David Armitage, *The Declaration of Independence: A Global History* (Cambridge: Harvard University Press, 2007).

8. Compare Felix Gilbert, *To the Farewell Address: Ideas of Early American Foreign Policy* (Princeton: Princeton University Press, 1961) with James H. Hutson, "Intellectual Foundations of Early American Diplomacy," *Diplomatic History* 1 (1977): 1–19.

9. See Jonathan R. Dull, *Franklin the Diplomat: The French Mission* (Philadelphia: American Philosophical Society, 1982 [as *Transactions* 72, part 1]), *A Diplomatic History of the American Revolution* (New Haven: Yale University Press, 1985), *Benjamin Franklin and the American Revolution* (Lincoln: University of Nebraska Press, 2010), and "Franklin Furioso, 1775–1790," in David Waldstreicher, ed., *A Companion to Benjamin Franklin* (Chichester UK: Wiley-Blackwell, 2011), 65–79; Gerald Stourzh, *Benjamin Franklin and American Foreign Policy*, 2nd ed. (Chicago: University of Chicago Press, 1969).

12. The Continental Army

1. See Piers Mackesy, *The Coward of Minden: The Affair of Lord George Sackville* (London: Allen Lane, 1979) and *The War for America, 1775–1783* (Cambridge: Harvard University Press, 1965), and N. A. M. Rodger, *The Insatiable Earl: A Life of John Montagu, Earl of Sandwich, 1718–1792* (London: HarperCollins, 1993).

2. Mackesy, *War for America*, 54–87.

3. Mackesy, *War for America*, 98–102; Daniel A. Baugh, "The Politics of British Naval Failure, 1775–1777," *American Neptune* 52 (1991): 221–46, and "Why Did Britain Lose Control of the Sea during the War for America," in Black and Woodfine, *British Navy*, 155–56; Robert T. Aggarwala, "'One such place in North America': New York, Boston, and Halifax as British Naval Bases, 1743–1783," *Northern Mariner* 23 (2013): 357.

4. George Athan Billias, *General John Glover and His Marblehead Mariners* (New York: Henry Holt, 1960); Ferling, *Almost a Miracle*, 1–11, 120–55.

5. James L. Nelson, *Benedict Arnold's Navy: The Ragtag Fleet That Lost the Battle of Lake Champlain but Won the American Revolution* (Camden ME: McGraw-Hill, 2006).

6. David Hackett Fischer, *Washington's Crossing* (New York: Oxford University Press, 2004); Phillip Thomas Tucker, *George Washington's Surprise Attack: A New Look at the Battle That Decided the Fate of America* (New York: Skyhorse, 2014). For Cornwallis see Franklin B. and Mary Wickwire, *Cornwallis: The American Adventure* (Boston: Houghton Mifflin, 1970).

1. For Franklin's arrival in France, see Labaree, *Papers of Benjamin Franklin*, 23: xlix–lvii; Dull, *Franklin the Diplomat*, 14–24, and *Benjamin Franklin and the American Revolution*, 64–72.

2. For his landlord, see Thomas J. Schaeper, *France and America in the Revolutionary Era: The Life of Jacques-Donatien Leray de Chaumont, 1725-1803* (Providence R I: Berghahn Books, 1995). Franklin may have met privately with Diderot: Philipp Blom, *A Wicked Company: The Forgotten Radicalism of the European Enlightenment* (New York: Basic Books, 2010), 285–89.

3. Dull, *French Navy and American Independence*, 72–80, and *Franklin the Diplomat*, 22–25; Labaree, *Papers of Benjamin Franklin*, 24:243–45; William Bell Clark, *Lambert Wickes, Sea Raider and Diplomat: The Story of a Naval Captain of the Revolution* (New Haven: Yale University Press; London: Humphrey Milford, Oxford University Press, 1932).

4. Labaree, *Papers of Benjamin Franklin*, 25:207–14.

5. Mackesy, *War for America*, 105–30; Ferling, *Almost a Miracle*, 242–58; Stephen R. Taaffe, *The Philadelphia Campaign, 1777-1778* (Lawrence: University of Kansas Press, 2003); John W. Jackson, *The Pennsylvania Navy, 1775-1781: The Defense of the Delaware* (New Brunswick N J: Rutgers University Press, 1974).

6. Mintz, *Generals of Saratoga*, 69–233; Ferling, *Almost a Miracle*, 204–41; Mackesy, *War for America*, 130–44.

7. Labaree, *Papers of Benjamin Franklin*, 25:97–99, 234–37.

8. Dull, *French Navy and American Independence*, 83–89.

9. Dull, *French Navy and American Independence*, 351–53, 360.

10. For the following paragraphs, see Labaree, *Papers of Benjamin Franklin*, 25:240, 260–61, 282–85, 305–9, 401–4, 412, 419–24, 435–40; Benjamin Franklin Stevens, ed., *Facsimiles of Manuscripts in European Archives Relating to America, 1775-1783*, 25 vols. (London: privately printed, 1889–98), 21: no. 1831, quoted in Dull, *Franklin the Diplomat*, 30n; Dull, *Benjamin Franklin and the American Revolution*, 72–76, and *French Navy and American Independence*, 89–94, 103–4, 113, 117, 127.

11. Labaree, *Papers of Benjamin Franklin*, 23:96–99.

12. For a different interpretation about the impact of the Bavarian crisis, see John Hardman and Munro Price, eds., *Louis XVI and the Comte de Vergennes: Correspondence, 1774-1787* (Oxford: Voltaire Foundation, 1998), 3–154.

13. Labaree, *Papers of Benjamin Franklin*, 25:583–626, prints the treaties.

14. Spain Joins the War

1. Dull, *French Navy and American Independence*, 104-5, 359-60; Labaree, *Papers of Benjamin Franklin*, 26:138-42.

2. Dull, *French Navy and American Independence*, 108-12, 360. For Gérard's diplomatic mission, see Joseph Meng, ed., *Conrad Alexandre Gérard: Despatches and Instructions* (Baltimore: Johns Hopkins University Press, 1935).

3. Dull, *French Navy and American Independence*, 110; Mackesy, *War for America*, 190-202; Rodger, *Insatiable Earl*, 271-75; N. A. M. Rodger, *The Command of the Ocean: A Naval History of Britain, 1649-1815* (London: Allen Lane, 2004), 335-36.

4. Mackesy, *War for America*, 196-202; Ferling, *Almost a Miracle*, 308-13; Dull, *French Navy and American Independence*, 122-24; William Laird Clowes, *The Royal Navy: A History from the Earliest Times to the Present*, 7 vols. (Boston: Little, Brown, 1897-1903), 3:397-412; David Syrett, *Admiral Lord Howe: A Biography* (Annapolis: Naval Institute Press, 2006), 49-108.

5. Dull, *French Navy and American Independence*, 106-7, 123-24; Mackesy, *War for America*, 213-19, 225-32; Ferling, *Almost a Miracle*, 294-308; Rodger, *Command of the Sea*, 339; Clowes, *Royal Navy*, 3:426-30.

6. Dull, *French Navy and American Independence*, 116-22; David Syrett, *The Royal Navy in European Waters during the American Revolutionary War* (Columbia: University of South Carolina Press, 1998), 48-59; Mackesy, *War for America*, 210-11, 237-43; Rodger, *Insatiable Earl*, 241-55; Clowes, *Royal Navy*, 3:412-26; Emmanuel-Henri, vicomte de Grouchy, and Paul Cottin, eds., *Journal inédit du duc de Croÿ, 1718-84*, 4 vols. (Paris: Flammarion, 1906-7), 4:125-27.

7. Dull, *French Navy and American Independence*, 359-63.

8. John Walton Caughey, *Bernardo de Gálvez in Louisiana, 1776-1783* (Berkeley: University of California Press, 1934).

9. Dull, *French Navy and American Independence*, 110-18, 126-34.

10. Dull, *French Navy and American Independence*, 129-43.

15. Spain Might Have Made Peace

1. The fullest account of the attempt to invade England is A. Temple Patterson, *The Other Armada: The Franco-Spanish Attempt to Invade England in 1779* (Manchester: Manchester University Press, 1960), but see also Dull, *French Navy and American Independence*, 143-58, Rodger, *Insatiable Earl*, 257-63, and Mackesy, *War for America*, 279-97.

2. John D. Harbron, *Trafalgar and the Spanish Navy* (London: Conway Maritime Press; Annapolis: Naval Institute Press, 1988), 50-76.

3. Dull, *American Naval History*, 24-26, and *French Navy and American Independence*, 158n; Jean Boudriot, *John Paul Jones and the* Bonhomme Richard: *A Reconstruction of the Ship and an Account of the Battle with* HMS Serapis, trans. David H. Roberts (Annapolis: Naval Institute Press, 1987); Thomas J. Schaeper, *John Paul Jones and the Battle off Flamborough Head* (New York: Peter Lang, 1989).

4. Dull, *French Navy and American Independence*, 169-79; Mackesy, *War for America*, 309-13, 319-23. For Rodney see Peter Trew, *Rodney and the Breaking of the Line* (Barnsley UK: Pen and Sword, 2006).

5. Ferling, *Almost a Miracle*, 303-25, 352-55, 384-90; Nash, *Unknown American Revolution*, 345-58; Max M. Mintz, *Seeds of Empire: The American Revolutionary Conquest of the Iroquois* (New York: New York University Press, 1999); Alexander A. Lawrence, *Storm over Savannah: The Story of Count d'Estaing and the Siege of the Town in 1779* (Athens: University of Georgia Press, 1951).

6. Labaree, *Papers of Benjamin Franklin*, 31:370-71n; Dull, *French Navy and American Independence*, 190; Stanley J. Idzerda, ed., *Lafayette in the Age of the American Revolution: Selected Letters and Papers, 1776-1790*, 5 vols. to date (Ithaca: Cornell University Press, 1972-), 2:313-19, 344-49.

7. Dull, *French Navy and American Independence*, 181-83; Mackesy, *War for America*, 323-34, 346-49; Clowes, *Royal Navy*, 3:456-71; Admiral de Guichen to Sartine, July 9, 1780, French Foreign Ministry Archives, Political Correspondence, Spain, vol. 599, pp. 389-95.

8. Mackesy, *War for America*, 357-59, 375; Dull, *French Navy and American Independence*, 193-94.

16. West Point

1. Willcox, *Portrait of a General*, 203-309; John A. Tilley, *The British Navy and the American Revolution* (Columbia: University of South Carolina Press, 1987), 163-89.

2. Ferling, *Almost a Miracle*, 416-28; William B. Willcox, ed., *The American Rebellion: Sir Henry Clinton's Narrative of His Campaigns, 1775-1782, with an Appendix of Original Documents* (New Haven: Yale University Press, 1954), 157-72; Charles P. Borick, *A Gallant Defense: The Siege of Charleston, 1780* (Columbia: University of South Carolina Press, 2005).

3. Ferling, *Almost a Miracle*, 435-36.

4. David Syrett, *The Royal Navy in American Waters, 1775-1783* (Aldershot UK and Brookfield VT: Scolar Press, 1989), 145-54. For Arnold see James Kirby Martin, *Benedict Arnold, Revolutionary Hero: An Amer-*

ican Warrior Reconsidered (New York: New York University Press, 1997) and Willard Sterne Randall, *Benedict Arnold, Patriot and Traitor* (New York: William Morrow, 1990).

5. Nash, *Unknown American Revolution*, 157–66, 320–39; Sylvia Frey, *Water from the Rock: Black Resistance in a Revolutionary Age* (Princeton: Princeton University Press, 1991); Ronald Hoffman, Thad W. Tate, and Peter J. Albert, eds., *An Uncivil War: The Southern Backcountry during the American Revolution* (Charlottesville: University Press of Virginia, 1985); John Buchanan, *The Road to Guilford Court House: The American Revolution in the Carolinas* (New York: John Wiley and Sons, 1997).

17. Possible Financial Collapse

1. Labaree, *Papers of Benjamin Franklin*, 23:469–70.

2. Robert A. Becker, "Currency, Taxation, and Finance, 1775–1787," in Greene and Pole, *Companion to the American Revolution*, 388–97; E. James Ferguson, *The Power of the Purse: A History of American Public Finance, 1776–1790* (Chapel Hill: University of North Carolina Press, 1961); Richard Buel Jr., *In Irons: Britain's Naval Supremacy and the American Revolutionary Economy* (New Haven: Yale University Press, 1998).

3. Labaree, *Papers of Benjamin Franklin*, 32:573–74, 587–88, 619–20, 625–27; 33:52–53, 141–42, 145. For Adams's checkered diplomatic career, see James H. Hutson, *John Adams and the Diplomacy of the American Revolution* (Lexington: University Press of Kentucky, 1980).

4. Labaree, *Papers of Benjamin Franklin*, 37:633–40; 39:160–61n, 201–5.

5. Dull, *French Navy and American Independence*, 345–50.

6. J. F. Bosher, *French Finances, 1770–1795: From Business to Bureaucracy* (Cambridge: Cambridge University Press, 1970); Robert D. Harris, *Necker, Reform Statesman of the Ancien Regime* (Berkeley: University of California Press, 1979).

7. Dull, *Age of the Ship of the Line*, 183, and *French Navy and American Independence*, 350n. For British financing of the American war, see Stephen Conway, *The British Isles and the War of American Independence* (New York: Oxford University Press, 2000), 51–54, 76–77, 106.

8. Dull, *French Navy and American Independence*, 194–202.

9. For a fuller critique, see Dull, *French Navy and American Independence*, 202.

10. Labaree, *Papers of Benjamin Franklin*, 39:203n.

11. Dull, *French Navy and American Independence*, 349.

12. Dull, *French Navy and American Independence*, 213–14.

13. Labaree, *Papers of Benjamin Franklin*, 37:635–40; 39:201–5.

14. Wayne E. Carp, *To Starve the Army at Pleasure: Continental Army Administration and American Political Culture, 1775-1783* (Chapel Hill: University of North Carolina Press, 1984).

15. For a summary, see Nash, *Unknown American Revolution*, 357-65.

16. See Ferling, *Almost a Miracle*, 476-500, 507-16, and Willcox, *Portrait of a General*, 347-91.

18. Cooperation Needed for Victory

1. Isabel de Madariaga, *Britain, Russia, and the Armed Neutrality of 1780: Sir James Harris's Mission to St. Petersburg during the American Revolution* (New Haven: Yale University Press, 1962) provides a perceptive account.

2. Dull, *French Navy and American Independence*, 206-8, 256-57; Syrett, *Royal Navy in European Waters*, 125-32.

3. Scott, *British Foreign Policy in the Age of the American Revolution*, 284-306.

4. Dull, *French Navy and American Independence*, 290-91, 372; Clowes, *Royal Navy*, 3:505-9; Syrett, *Royal Navy in European Waters*, 95-132.

5. Dull, *French Navy and American Independence*, 222-24; Mackesy, *War for America*, 386-96.

6. Labaree, *Papers of Benjamin Franklin*, 34:433-34. For Colonel Laurens, see Gregory D. Massey, *John Laurens and the American Revolution* (Columbia: University of South Carolina Press, 2002). Castries's account of the meeting makes it clear he believed de Grasse should extend his stay in North America: French Naval Archives, B⁴216: 196-98, Castries to Vergennes, March 11, 1781.

7. Dull, *French Navy and American Independence*, 247-49.

8. Clowes, *Royal Navy*, 3:483-88 summarizes the 1781 campaign in the West Indies.

9. For the ensuing Yorktown campaign, see Willcox, *Portrait of a General*, 392-494; Dull, *French Navy and American Independence*, 238-49; Mackesy, *War for America*, 416-30; Ferling, *Almost a Miracle*, 523-39; Howard C. Rice and Anne S. K. Brown, eds., *The American Campaigns of Rochambeau's Army, 1780, 1781, 1782, 1783*, 2 vols. (Princeton: Princeton University Press and Providence: Brown University Press, 1972).

10. See Francisco Morales Padrón, ed., *Journal of Don Francisco Saavedra de Sangronis during the Commission He Had in His Charge from 25 June 1780 until the 20th of the Same Month of 1783*, trans. Aileen Moore Topping (Gainesville: University Press of Florida, 2009).

11. Colin Pengelly, *Sir Samuel Hood and the Battle of the Chesapeake* (Gainesville: University Press of Florida, 2009), 124–60, 227–29.

12. Buel, *In Irons*, 213–15.

13. Dull, *French Navy and American Independence*, 396–72 lists each ship and its location.

14. Dull, *French Navy and American Independence*, 234–36.

15. Ian R. Christie, *The End of North's Ministry, 1780–1782* (London: Macmillan, 1958), 363–69; Mackesy, *War for America*, 474.

16. Mackesy, *War for America*, 524–25.

19. The Peace Treaty

1. Labaree, *Papers of Benjamin Franklin*, 37:24–25. For Franklin's circle of female acquaintances and friends, see Claude-Anne Lopez, *Mon Cher Papa: Franklin and the Ladies of Paris* (New Haven: Yale University Press, 1966).

2. Labaree, *Papers of Benjamin Franklin*, 36:456–58, 504–6; 37:17–18, 24–25, 292–93.

3. For accounts of the negotiations, see Hoffman and Albert, *Peace and the Peacemakers*; Dull, *French Navy and American Independence*, 274–76, 288–335; Vincent T. Harlow, *The Founding of the Second British Empire, 1763–1793*, 2 vols. (London: Longman, Green, 1952–64), 1:362–407; Richard B. Morris, *The Peacemakers: The Great Powers and American Independence* (New York: Harper and Row, 1965); and Andrew Stockley, *Britain and France at the Birth of America: The European Powers and the Peace Negotiations of 1782–1783* (Exeter: Exeter University Press, 2001). For Shelburne's domestic policies, see John M. Norris, *Shelburne and Reform* (London: Macmillan, 1963).

4. Franklin kept a detailed journal of the first phase of the negotiations (through the end of June): Labaree, *Papers of Benjamin Franklin*, 37:291–346. For Oswald and the other British negotiators, see Charles R. Ritcheson, "Britain's Peacemakers, 1782–1783: 'To an Astonishing Degree Unfit for the Task'?" in Hoffman and Albert, *Peace and the Peacemakers*, 70–100.

5. Labaree, *Papers of Benjamin Franklin*, 37:169–72, 177–78, 295–97. For the congressional instructions to the peace commissioners, see William C. Stinchcombe, *The American Revolution and the French Alliance* (Syracuse: Syracuse University Press, 1969), 153–69.

6. Labaree, *Papers of Benjamin Franklin*, 37:309n, 313n, 316.

7. Labaree, *Papers of Benjamin Franklin*, 37:337, 341–42, 558–59.

8. See Scott, *British Foreign Policy in the Age of the American Revolution*, 320–27.

9. Labaree, *Papers of Benjamin Franklin*, 37:685n; 38:244n.

10. See Charles R. Ritcheson, "The Earl of Shelburne and Peace with America, 1782–1783: Vision and Reality," *International History Review* 5 (1983): 322–45.

11. See Bradford Perkins, "The Peace of Paris: Patterns and Legacies," in Hoffman and Albert, *Peace and the Peacemakers*, 190–229.

12. Dull, *French Navy and American Independence*, 251–302.

13. Labaree, *Papers of Benjamin Franklin*, 37:598–602.

14. Labaree, *Papers of Benjamin Franklin*, 37:686–87.

15. Labaree, *Papers of Benjamin Franklin*, 38:30–34, 113n.

16. Labaree, *Papers of Benjamin Franklin*, 37:712–13; 38:6–8, 82–83n, 92–93, 96–98, 122n, 132n, 164; Perkins, "Peace of Paris," 199–204. For Jay's lengthy career, see Walter Stahr, *John Jay, Founding Father* (New York: Hambledon, 2005).

17. Dull, "Vergennes, Rayneval, and the Diplomacy of Trust," 101–31.

18. For the crisis, see Alan W. Fisher, *The Russian Annexation of the Crimea, 1772–1783* (Cambridge: Cambridge University Press, 1970).

19. Labaree, *Papers of Benjamin Franklin*, 38:192n; Perkins, "Peace of Paris," 207–9.

20. Labaree, *Papers of Benjamin Franklin*, 38:220n, 272n, 275, 388, 451–52.

21. Labaree, *Papers of Benjamin Franklin*, 38:382–88.

22. For the following see Dull, *French Navy and American Independence*, 312–35.

23. James A. Lewis, *Neptune's Militia: The Frigate* South Carolina *during the American Revolution* (Kent, Ohio: Kent State University Press, 1999).

24. Labaree, *Papers of Benjamin Franklin*, 38:461–62, 464–66, 481, 487–89.

25. Labaree, *Papers of Benjamin Franklin*, 38:605–8.

20. The American Union

1. Labaree, *Papers of Benjamin Franklin*, 40:566–75.

2. Wells, "Population and Family," 41.

3. See Drew R. McCoy, *The Elusive Republic: Political Economy in Jeffersonian America* (Chapel Hill: University of North Carolina Press, 1980).

4. Jonathan R. Dull, "Two Republics in a Hostile World: The United States and the Netherlands in the 1780s," in Jack P. Greene, ed., *The American Revolution: Its Character and Limits* (New York: New York University Press, 1987), 149–63.

5. William M. Fowler Jr., *Jack Tars and Commodores: The American Navy, 1783-1814* (Boston: Houghton Mifflin, 1984), 1-16; E. Wayne Carp, "Demobilization and National Defense," in Greene and Pole, *Companion to the American Revolution*, 383-87, and "The Problem of National Defense in the Early American Republic," in Greene, *American Revolution*, 14-50.

6. For postwar relations with Britain, see Charles R. Ritcheson, *Aftermath of Revolution: British Policy towards the United States, 1783-1795* (Dallas: Southern Methodist University Press, 1969). For an overview of American foreign relations during the immediate postwar period, see Frederick W. Marks III, *Independence on Trial: Foreign Affairs and the Making of the Constitution* (Baton Rouge: Louisiana State University Press, 1973).

7. David Szatmary, *Shays' Rebellion: The Making of an American Insurrection* (Amherst: University of Massachusetts Press, 1980).

INDEX

Other works by Jonathan R. Dull

The French Navy and American Independence:
A Study of Arms and Diplomacy, 1774-1787
(Princeton: Princeton University Press, 1975)

Franklin the Diplomat: The French Mission
(Philadelphia: American Philosophical Society, 1982)

A Diplomatic History of the American Revolution
(New Haven: Yale University Press, 1985)

The French Navy and the Seven Years' War
(Lincoln: University of Nebraska Press, 2005)

The Age of the Ship of the Line: The British and French Navies,
1650-1815 (Lincoln: University of Nebraska Press, 2009)

Benjamin Franklin and the American Revolution
(Lincoln: University of Nebraska Press, 2010)

American Naval History, 1607-1865: Overcoming the Colonial Legacy
(Lincoln: University of Nebraska Press, 2012)

CPSIA information can be obtained at www.ICGtesting.com
Printed in the USA
LVOW06s2257021015

456674LV00001B/1/P